W9-BQT-114

Out of the fire—refined and purified—comes a story that will tug at your heartstrings and catapult you into the love and light of Christ, calling you to dance your own beautiful dance with the King of Creation.

—Kris Crawford
Disciple of Jesus Christ

In a culture that is allergic to suffering, it is difficult to come to terms with a God who permits loss and pain. *Dancing on My Ashes* tackles the theology of tragedy and grief through the testimony of two modern-day mourners who have found that faith, worship, and intimacy with God are born out of the valley of the shadow of the death—where the power of the resurrection rises out of the ashes of the fellowship of Christ's sufferings.

What *The Shack* did metaphorically, *Dancing on My Ashes* does with experience and reality. Surely the brokenhearted will find hope, life, and truth within the pages of this book.

—Zach Neese
Pastor of Worship Development
Gateway Church

The mark of an impactful story happens when the storyteller, unashamedly and courageously, bares her soul, inviting the reader to do the same. In *Dancing on My Ashes*, Holly and Heather not only share their story but help to walk the reader through the painful yet necessary healing process for when life deals us its harshest blows. *Dancing On My Ashes* soothes and empathizes with the broken heart, while sharing the truth of Scripture, and the hope that comes from the heart of God.

—Amena Brown
Performance poet and speaker

Dancing
ON MY ASHES

HEATHER GILION & HOLLY SNELL

learning to love the One who
gives and takes away

Dancing
ON MY ASHES

TATE PUBLISHING & *Enterprises*

Scripture quotations marked "NIV" are taken from the *Holy Bible, New International Version* ®, Copyright © 1973, 1978, 1984 by International Bible Society. Used by permission of Zondervan Publishing House. All rights reserved.

Scripture quotations marked "MSG" are taken from *The Message*, Copyright © 1993, 1994, 1995, 1996, 2000, 2001, 2002. Used by permission of NavPress Publishing Group. All rights reserved.

Scripture quotations marked "NLT" are taken from the Holy Bible, New Living Translation, Copyright © 1996. Used by permission of Tyndale House Publishers, Inc. All rights reserved.

Names, descriptions, entities, and incidents included in the story are based on the lives of real people.

The opinions expressed by the author are not necessarily those of Tate Publishing, LLC.

Published by Tate Publishing & Enterprises, LLC
127 E. Trade Center Terrace | Mustang, Oklahoma 73064 USA
1.888.361.9473 | www.tatepublishing.com

Tate Publishing is committed to excellence in the publishing industry. The company reflects the philosophy established by the founders, based on Psalm 68:11,
"The Lord gave the word and great was the company of those who published it."

Book design copyright © 2009 by Tate Publishing, LLC. All rights reserved.
Cover design by Kellie Southerland
Interior design by Stephanie Woloszyn
Cover Photo by Will Vastine Photography
Author Photos by Andrea Goings

Published in the United States of America

ISBN: 978-1-60799-871-6
1. Religion / Christian Life / Death, Grief, Bereavement
2. Religion / Christian Life / Inspirational
09.08.03

TABLE OF CONTENTS

Introduction

I WILL DANCE

Then maidens will dance and be glad. I will turn their mourning into gladness; I will give them comfort and joy instead of sorrow.

Jeremiah 31:13 (NIV)

David, wearing a linen ephod, danced before the Lord with all his might.

2 Samuel 6:14 (NIV)

I've never been a good dancer. My dancing debut came in second grade when I learned to square dance at school and promenaded with my crush around the gym floor dressed in my western garb. But my joy came with a price. I was so giddy about holding Ben's hand while promenading that I began giggling, and as some of you girls can relate, my nervous laughter led to the loss of control of my bladder. A square-dancing disaster and an embarrassing moment to share for years to come! I promenaded all over the floor—if you get my drift.

I have since then enjoyed dancing in the confines of my home. Occasionally, when no one is around, I will feel the urge, turn up the music, put some socks on my feet, and glide around on my hardwood floors. My dance is not polished or striking (unless you call dancing with your socks on polishing floors or hitting your hand on your kitchen counter while spinning around striking).

Why do we dance? My dances are more about a response than the actual choreography.

In May 2008 I spoke at a women's event called "The Awakening," and my sister Heidi and I also led worship for this two-day encounter weekend. After the first evening ended, our mom came up to me and said that while we were worshipping she had a flashback of me as a little girl dancing before the Lord. When I was four, I was first introduced to what David referred to as becoming "undignified" (2 Samuel 6:22) at Church on the Rock in Texas. This church began worship by saying, "Let the dancers come forth!" I was ready to dance! I'd grab my sister Holly and say, "Let's go!" As my mom watched me leading worship that Friday night, she wondered if I was going to break out in my dance. (For the visual reader, my dance as a four-year-old was simply a series of front kicks that lasted through all of the fast songs.)

That night I tossed and turned. I was speaking the next morning on some heavy topics, so my mind raced, and my heart desperately pleaded with the Lord to guide my thoughts and to continue to prepare my mind for what I was to share. I reminisced about the wounds that I had received on this journey and the beautiful scars of remembrance left in their place. I was so filled with awe over all that He had done for me that I was just about to explode. The Lord kept bringing me back to that memory of dancing as a little girl before Him. I remembered how I danced and how fun it felt and how even today that same feeling comes over me when I am worshipping Him. Sometimes I can't stand still, and I have to move. The urge now manifests itself in a more mature sway, but inside I am twirling and spinning and leaping all for my King.

The next morning, as I was closing my talk titled "Wounds and Scars," the memory of my dancing consumed my mind again. I started telling the story my mom had shared with me the night before, and I shared how it makes me feel to dance before Him today. In a moment I went from laughing to weeping as the Lord led me to say, "And now, I dance on these ashes—and they are beautiful."

I hadn't planned on saying that, but the Lord gave me a picture of what my worship looks like through His eyes. When I lift up my voice and sing to Him from deep within my being, He sees my praise and adoration as twirling and spinning and leaping in these ashes of despair, loneliness, solitude, desperation, and weakness. My world once came to an end and went up in flames, but even with my face to the ground and buried in my ashes, He called me to stand and stand firm in my ashes. He has taken my hand, raised me up, and asked me to dance. *May I have this dance?* He sees my melodic movements as adoration and praise that my lips may not be able to say on their own. It is worship from the deepest of places. This expression flows with each turn and sings with every whirl. He has led me in this dance to demonstrate His power in resurrecting a life that was once dead but is now alive and free—ready to dance! There is a time for everything. I mourned in my ashes. Now I dance on them!

> There is a time for everything...a time to weep and a time to laugh, a time to mourn and a time to dance.
>
> *Ecclesiastes 3:1,4 (NIV)*

My declaration that afternoon to dance was not only for me. After the event, two separate women stopped me and said, "Heather, when you said that you dance on your ashes, that was for me." God is so beyond little ole me! I hadn't planned on saying that—it wasn't in my notes. The Lord wanted others to hear it, and He used me as a vessel to declare the possibilities for one's ashes.

MY ASHES

In Scripture, ashes are used for many things. God first uses ashes to describe *us* in Genesis. Abraham speaks to the Lord and finds himself, on one hand, speaking directly to God Almighty, but on the other, recognizing who he is without God: nothing but dust and ashes (Genesis 18:27). Here Abraham humbled himself before his Creator prior to petitioning Him to act.

The second use for ashes shows up in Scripture in reference to sacrifices. We see numerous accounts of animal ashes used symbolically in the covering of sins. The unclean were commanded to put ashes from the burned purification offering into a jar and pour fresh water over them (Numbers 19:17, NIV).

And the third use of ashes is in mourning.

> Tamar put *ashes* on her head and tore her long-sleeved garment, which was on her; and she put her hand on her head and went away, crying aloud as she went.
>
> *2 Samuel 13:19 (NIV)*

> When Mordecai learned of all that had been done, he tore his clothes, put on sackcloth and ashes, and went out into the city, wailing loudly and bitterly.
>
> *Esther 4:1 (NIV)*

> Then Job took a piece of broken pottery and scraped himself with it as he sat among the ashes.
>
> *Job 2:8 (NIV)*

Ashes are the remains of something that has been destroyed by fire, and they were used as dust on the grieving to symbolize a time of mourning. Ashes were a sign of humility and sorrow. In addition to ashes, the Israelites wore sackcloth to show others they were mourning. Joseph Jacobs in his book, *Sackcloth,* says sackcloth, a fabric resembling burlap, was a "coarsely woven fabric, usually made of goat's hair. It...was chiefly worn as a token of mourning by the Israelites. It was furthermore a sign of submission."[1]

The Israelites placed ashes on their heads as a sign to show that they were in mourning, that some great disaster had fallen upon them, or that they had received a message of punishment from God because of their disobedience and waywardness. They were after repentance and, as an act of submission, used sackcloth and ashes as an outward display of their pain and sorrow. We may try hard to hide our pain or our season of grieving today, but for the Israelites, it was a public affair. "No one could miss someone who was in mourning! And needless to say, people who walked around wearing sackcloth, and with ashes all through their hair, were not the most beautiful sight."[2]

Jesus spoke to those wearing sackcloth and ashes too, and He offered them more than painful garb or the remains to life's destruction: "To all who mourn in Israel, he will give a crown of beauty for ashes, a joyous blessing instead of mourning, festive praise instead of despair" (Isaiah 61:3 NLT).

Jesus singled out the grieving by inviting them to exchange their ashes for a crown—a crown of beauty. When Jesus first made it clear who He was and what He came to do, He stood before those gathered in the temple on the Sabbath and read from the book of Isaiah. He spoke to the brokenhearted and to those who mourned, to those in captivity and to the needy. He brought good news to the poor and comfort to the brokenhearted, and He proclaimed that captives would be released and that prisoners would be freed. He declared that the time of the Lord's favor had come (Luke 4:18–19).

Today His mission remains! Not only was He sent to those who walked the streets with Him two thousand years ago; He has been sent to us in the here and now. He walks the road with us today and will journey with generations to come. His mission to meet us in the ashes is as true today as it was in His first declaration.

If you find yourself covered in the remains of life-as-you-knew-it, I am speaking to you. Ecclesiastes is clear: there is a time for *everything*. My friend, there is a time to mourn, there is a time to cry, there is a time to wail, and there is a time to sit in a pile of ashes. But you don't have to stay there! There is a time to raise your head and see that He is near. There is a time to dust off the ashes that cover your brow and accept His presentation of your new crown, a crown called beauty. No longer do you mourn, covered in ashes. No longer do you feel forgotten. Christ has declared, "I have been sent to tell those who mourn that the time of the Lord's favor has come" (Isaiah 6:2).

> For His anger is but for a moment, His favor is for a lifetime;
>> Weeping may last for the night, But a shout of joy comes in the morning.
>
> *Psalm 30:5 (NASB)*

One day the sorrowful tears that you shed will be replaced with tears of gratitude and thankfulness. Your heart will shout and even dance as you wear your crown as a covering of beauty. It won't happen automatically or without purposeful choosing, so the dance is up to you; and it begins with accepting His invitation—an invitation to look up and behold that He has the power to make your ashes and remains a cause of celebration, a source of beauty, and a reason to dance. *He* is your reason. When you see Him—truly see Him—you will rise, and you will stand firmly planted. Your kingdom, the kingdom you may have built with your own two hands, will be under your feet, but you'll stand with arms held high to your King. And, my friend, there will come a day when you will dance! With everything in you, you will dance! Will everything be replaced and glorious? It won't matter, because if you have Him, you have *everything!*

> David…danced before the LORD with all his might.
>
> *2 Samuel 6:14 (NIV)*

We are ready to dance over the ashes of our lives because we serve a God that has truly made beauty from ashes.

—Holly Snell

My sister Holly and I write this book not because our journey in life has been more difficult than yours but simply because it is our dance. We have wept. We have laughed. We have mourned. We have danced. We now invite you to come along with us on this journey into our ashes, and more importantly, into our dance.

Remembering My Kingdom

CHILDLIKE FAITH

Do you remember the moment you saw Him? The exact moment your eyes met, and you knew in that second you were forever changed? Do you remember the moment He saw you—right through you? There was no place to hide, no use in cowering, for your heart and your thoughts were laid bare before His eyes. He knew your name, and as He spoke it, everything in you melted, even the very thing that you thought you had protected—your hardened heart.

When I encountered this living God, my world was destroyed. All I once knew about this God became fairy tales and fables, and a man like no other emerged from the fire. But was He a man at all? The smoke around Him was so thick from the flames that consumed my world that I couldn't make out His face, but I knew that He was coming toward me. He was coming *for* me.

Could He be the one to rescue me from these flames? Then again, wasn't He the one who had caused the blaze, the heat, this destruction? Caught in His path, I was frozen with fear—not the fear that makes you hide, but the kind that makes you defenseless. I was helpless as I fell to my knees. That was the moment I knew my world was at its end. As the smoke cleared, and my eyes beheld His throne, the veil was torn, and He beckoned me to come into the Holy of Holies.

As the song says, "This is my story; this is my song." In this story, my world collided with His, and for a mere moment, I was face-to-face with God. Scripture speaks that no one can see His face and live. This is true; I had to die. This crisis brought my kingdom—the kingdom I had created and built with my two hands—to mere ashes in an instant. I stood before a king; let me rephrase that: I stood before *the* King. And inside this King's kingdom, what He says goes. My moment before the King was a day of reckoning— a reckoning and wrecking of my life as I knew it. On an altar before me, everything I valued was consumed before my very eyes; but as one died that day, another was brought to life.

I laid myself—my weaknesses and my doubts— bare before me in this feeble attempt to communicate my moment of death to you. Fear tries to make his home in my heart, but fear may not reside there, for

God ordained this journey for me to partake in and for you to witness. He longs for you to see Him so much so that He woke this servant in the middle of the night to begin telling a story. This is a love story of God loving me so much that He would allow me to experience great pain and great loss to lose everything yet gain my soul. This love didn't care about reputation; He didn't care about my living out laws. Love cared enough to save me from myself and became the offer I couldn't refuse. I couldn't run fast enough, or hide far enough, and I couldn't put Him in a box and save Him for later. This unmerited, abounding, extravagant love answered my questions of who and why.

I tell you this story in faith, not to glorify my name, but to make much of one name: the name of Jesus Christ. This journey that unravels before you will be one of a terrific triumph over tragedy, a heart-wrenching surrender, and an unforgettable journey to His heights. A journey—I must add—I'm still on. This is my journey of pursuit and death, and I pray that this story will not be merely a story but an invitation for you to see the Lord too.

He longs to write our story. The Lord has the characters all in place; He knows the twists and turns, and He knows the moment when all else will fade away, and we will be faced with the face of Christ. What He does with us will be up to Him, but what we do next will be up to us. Stepping out of our kingdoms and into His—that is our journey. The kingdom of God is at hand! The King is calling for you. Do you hear Him? He's calling your name.

The Lord called my name at a very young age. I knew His name and knew I went to church to sing and hear about Him. Around the dinner table we thanked Him, and when in need, we called for Him. There was a picture of Him in our living room, so I knew what He looked like; His face was rugged but kind, strong but gentle, powerful but approachable. This was my God.

My dad and mom knew Him well. When they spoke of Him, they spoke with trust that He was alive and active and listening to our prayers to get us through all obstacles and hardships. He was our joy, and He made us sing and rejoice over the blessings He had poured on us. He was the song that played in our home, in our car, and in our hearts. He was our life.

While I was growing up, we struggled financially and were sometimes in the position to pray that God would provide our next meal. Sure enough, right when we needed it, not a minute too late, groceries were delivered or a kind, generous donor would fund our trip to the supermarket. God *was* alive and active, and as a child I knew He was at church, but I knew He was with the Wall family too.

I preface the story of my salvation with this side note. My dad and I had a special relationship. He had high hopes for a son he could nickname Bubba, and the moment my parents knew they were expecting their second child my dad started calling me Bubba. I think he believed if he spoke out of faith he would get the boy that he had been hoping for. Well, out I came, and although I had no boy parts, my name remained: I was Bubba.

Before I could read, I asked Christ to "come live in my heart." I didn't quite comprehend what I was asking for or even how that was possible, but I knew He existed even if I couldn't see Him. I knew there was a "Him," and so far I really liked Him. I was told that I could simply tell Him I was sorry for my "sins": the time I lied to my parents and I really *had* taken my friend's Barbie doll hair dryer, the times I got mad at my sisters and called them poo-poo heads, or the time I decided not to share my Cabbage Patch Doll, Melody, with my cousin, or when I told Heidi to "shut-up!" For everything I had done that displeased Him, I could ask Him to forgive me and invite Him to come make His home in me. I also didn't quite know what that would require, and if I did, I might have thought twice about the cost. But in my four-year-old little world, I knew He had to be mine, so one Sunday in children's church, I raised my tiny hand, repeated a simple prayer, and in seconds I was pronounced "saved." The teachers said I had to tell other people that my name was now recorded in the Book of Life, so I was ushered into *big* service that day because our church thought it was a good idea to share these decisions with everyone. As the preacher finished giving an invitation, those of us who had made decisions for Christ stood up front so we could celebrate with the entire church family. Cheers rang out that another child had given her heart to Jesus, and they asked me, "Can you tell everyone your name?"

"Bubba Wall," I said shyly. And as my two embarrassed parents approached the stage, delight took over because they knew their little girl got it. She got that she needed Jesus, and my parents got that maybe they should call me Heather for a while. But I'm certain that I'll need to remember to ask the angel to look up "Bubba Wall" in the Book of Life.

Holly's my big sister with only three years that separate us. She had her first God encounter at an early age as well.

Holly

"Holly, Holly, get up." I stirred a little in my bed. When I was only five years old, I heard Him call my name. We lived in a small town nestled between Kansas City and Jefferson City, Missouri, in a modest apartment that sat underneath a water tower that looked like an eight ball from a pool table. "Holly, Holly, get up." I ignored the voice once again. Finally, a third time, "Holly, Holly, get up." I removed the covers from my body and hazily proceeded to my parents' room. "Dad, what do you want?" He didn't answer right away. He rubbed his eyes and rolled over to look at me. "Dad, what do you want?"

He looked at me and said, "Holly, go back to bed. I didn't call you."

I turned and headed back to my room and quickly fell right back to sleep. I don't know how much time passed, but I was awakened once again by the same voice. "Holly, Holly, get up." Getting out of bed much quicker this time, I set off for my parent's room. "Dad, what do you want?"

"Holly, I did not call you."

"But I heard you. You told me to get up."

Dad sat up this time and pulled me close to say, "Holly, I did not call you, but if you hear the voice again, you need to say, 'Lord, I am here. Speak to me.'"

I, of course, went back to bed but did not go back to sleep right away. Even at the age of five, I knew about Jesus. I understood as much as I could at that age about the sacrifice He paid for me. I didn't hear His voice again that night, but I knew it had been the Lord. I remember lying there in my bed with the moonlight casting shadows over my room. I sensed His presence. I knew that He was real.

The next morning Dad sat me down, and we discussed the night before. He told me about the story of Samuel, and he shared with me how Hannah, Samuel's mother, had prayed for a child. She was barren, but the Lord granted her request and blessed her with Samuel. As he grew older and was serving Eli the priest, Samuel had an encounter with God.

One night Eli, who was almost blind by now, had just gone to bed. The lamp of God had not yet gone out, and Samuel was sleeping in the Tabernacle near the Ark of God. Suddenly, the Lord called out, "Samuel! Samuel!"

"Yes?" Samuel replied. "What is it?" He jumped up and ran to Eli. "Here I am. What do you need?"

"I didn't call you," Eli replied. "Go on back to bed." So he did. This happened two more times. On the third time, Eli realized it was the Lord calling the boy. So he said to Samuel, "Go and lie down again, and if someone calls again, say 'Yes, Lord, your servant is listening.'"

1 Samuel 3:2–9 (NLT)

The Lord was calling to me that night. My dad, understanding this, knew it was time for me to respond to His call, and he prayed with me to accept Jesus as my personal Savior that day.

Don't get me wrong, I was still very much a "normal" oldest child who at times found pleasure in tormenting my younger sisters, but I can honestly say that I had a true relationship with my Creator that was so very real and precious to me.

Permit the children to come to Me, do not hinder them; for the kingdom of God belongs to such as these. Truly I say to you, whoever does not receive the kingdom of God like a child will not enter it at all.

Mark 10:14–15 (NAS)

As children we see God in others, and we are able to see good in most everything until we are shown otherwise. I was surrounded by goodness. My mom came from a family who loved the Lord, and they lived it. My grandparents were active in their church and continue to be. My grandpa was the worship leader and sang in the choir, my grandma played the organ, and my great-grandma always swapped books with my dad as they spoke of the great depths of the Lord. Everywhere I went, God became real through these people. No, I couldn't see His face, but I was confident of His existence.

God also became alive to me through the work of His hands in creation. I can look back and hear His voice telling me, "Do you see those stars? I did that!" During the many trips we made to and from my grandparents house, while we cruised the big highway, I would look out the window at the evening sky and bask in His glory. The sky was so big and the stars so brilliant that wonder rose and awe developed within my little heart.

I recall a warm spring day when I wandered over to a tree that sat in-between my grandparents' and my great-grandma's houses. I wanted to sing to Him, and as I clung to the tree's trunk, I twirled 'round and 'round, singing of this Creator. At that moment, His child stood within His kingdom, blessing the King and loving her Jesus. She wasn't consumed with the worries of this world and had faith that He was who He said He was. I danced before Him without wondering who might see me or what they might think. It was just one girl loving her one God. I didn't have to see Him—I felt Him.

I wish I could say that I was never hindered by what others thought of my love for Him, but sadly enough, He fades out as we let other things fade in. Soon it became harder and harder for me to stand in the middle of His creation, dancing and singing before His throne. It became more difficult for me to simply stand for Him at all. Teen years approached, and my relationship with God resembled less of Him making His home in my heart and more of my asking Him to stay in His room until the coast was clear. I cared what friends at school thought of me, I cared what friends at church thought of me, and I cared more about everyone else's opinion than what God thought of me. I was a good girl—a Christian girl—in a Christian family, with parents that worked in the church. When the doors were open, we were there. Why? I guess because we were the ones with the keys. My dad was on staff as the outreach minister, and my mom was the church secretary. We were the Wall Family: Evan and Diane with their kids: Holly, Heather, Heidi, Heath, and Hannah (Hunter would soon be on the way). My reputation was safe because of the reputation of our family.

In those years I occasionally let God near, but more frequently I kept Him far. I did my best to push Him away, all the while keeping Him within arms reach—I didn't know when I might need something. I placed my attention on other distractions, and it was easier to *play* church than *be* the church. But then tragedy struck and overnight I was faced with the fear of the loss of life as I knew it.

I awoke to find that my dad had been taken to the hospital during the night because he had suffered a stroke. When we were taken to the hospital to see him after school, nothing could have prepared me as I walked into his room. Wires were strung everywhere, machines beeped, and one question rang through my mind: Who is this man lying before me? This was the beginning of some serious questions that reeled in my fourteen-year-old mind. Why is *my* dad sick? He's a good guy, why is this bad thing happening to him? Can I ever have back what I had before?

But God showed up and showed off. Our family believed God would do a miracle, and we witnessed my mom's pleading with God, trusting God, and leaning on God. Looking back, I see a strength that resonated through her that could only have been Christ stepping in and taking over. During those unforgettably heart-wrenching days, she was strong, never doubted, and was always full of trust and hope that God would restore our father. There were surgeries with painful reports that he wouldn't make it through the night, and doctors informed us that even if he did live, Dad would never walk or eat a normal meal again. Those who reviewed his charts and performed his surgeries gave us little hope, but my dad didn't believe this was the end; he believed God was placing faith within his heart to trust and believe Him for a healing.

During this turbulent time, I visited Dad in the hospital with my mom, and he shared with us what seemed to me a frightening experience. He told us that he felt himself dying the night before and that he felt like his spirit was beginning to leave his body, but he had cried out to the Lord for help. He felt the Lord speak to his heart, "I will take care of you whether you live or die."

He had such peace and relief that gleamed from his face that day, but inside it was the first time I realized that my dad was not immortal.

Heather

Dad improved. His doctors were always surprised but cautioned us to not be too excited about the positives. They wanted to protect us, and they encouraged us to live in "reality"; however, I was learning that reality belongs to God and God alone. After four long months, he was released from the hospital. Though the doctors weren't quite sure he was ready, my dad was ready; after all, it was Thanksgiving.

And we were thankful. While he was in the hospital, all he talked about and all he dreamed for was home. *Home* is a sweet word that most of us take for granted, but for a long-term hospital patient, home is priceless. He was still *very* sick, yet *very* determined to not go back to the hospital. Within a few weeks of being home, he came down with shingles, blood clots formed in his body that cut off circulation to his left fingertips, and he lost a major amount of blood, but he still refused to go back. After only five weeks at home, his body had finally had enough, and he collapsed and was rushed back to the hospital. The doctors assured us it was a miracle that he was still alive, for he had lost three-fourths of his blood and had nearly hemorrhaged to death. He had a massive blood transfusion, and the fingertips on his left hand had to be amputated, but the worst part, Dad would say, was that he was in the hospital again.

By that time we were getting used to him being there, and the routine of running home, to school, to the hospital, and to church became our new normal. Thoughts crossed my mind of life without my dad, but my mom would quickly reassure us that he was going to make it. God was on our side! Our spirits would pick back up, and we would press on.

A new problem evolved that required surgery. Over a ten- to fifteen-year period, a fistula had formed that caused stomach acid to seep through a faulty valve and burned a hole through Dad's esophagus. Because of the bleeding that had occurred he needed surgery yet again. The night before the surgery, the doctor came into Dad's hospital room and said, "Evan, we can't do the surgery. We've got a problem." When Dad first came to the hospital for his stroke and then again when he nearly hemorrhaged to death, we thought we had hit rock bottom, but this time rock bottom actually came.

"Evan, the lab checked and double-checked the blood tests and found that you've contracted HIV."

Even now I struggle to find the words to describe what went through my mind at that moment. With news like this, you ask, "How do we hope now? How do we believe when what we're facing is an incurable disease?" This mountain seemed so much larger than the last.

Dad explained to the doctors that he was a heterosexual and that he was a virgin when he got married; he didn't understand how this could have happened. The doctors said it must have been contracted by a blood transfusion, and they left us with this statement: "The harsh reality is you may have a month—a year—maybe five years, but you will die of AIDS eventually." We were stunned. Why would God bring him through so much to have him die of a virus that wasn't his fault?

He was failing physically, but one doctor did what no one else would: he performed the surgery. But after the surgery, everything seemed to go wrong. His heart failed. His last kidney failed. The doctors put him on dialysis and it failed. His lungs, heart rate, and blood pressure all showed bad signs. The doctors told my mom there was no hope for Dad's survival.

But as small as it was, hope still remained.

I stood by and watched as many cried, "God, where are you?" (I've since learned that there are some questions we flippantly ask God, and if we gathered to whom we are talking, we might hold our tongues a great deal more than we do.) We asked God where He was. He indeed heard our question, and He was ready to reply!

The church began praying, and I remember that one specific evening the entire church cancelled the Sunday night services for the sole purpose of going to God on behalf of my dad. People wept, begged, pleaded, and worshiped God. That night someone spoke out in belief that God was saying clearly that He was more than able to heal a man in a hospital bed.

Faith took root in our hearts. I knew that God was aware and He was able.

> If you have faith the size of a mustard seed, you will
> say to this mountain, "Move from here to there,"
> and it will move; and nothing will be impossible
> to you.
>
> *Matthew 17:20 (NAS)*

Prayer lines at the church began to fire up. His name
was broadcast over a local Christian radio station. My
dad's mother and stepfather made it to the hospital.
They didn't know much about the miracle-working
power of Jesus, but his mom challenged the Lord on
a Sunday morning when his health was deteriorating:
"God, if there's a change in Evan this morning, we'll go
to church." God heard that prayer, and within minutes
the dialysis began to work. My mom made them keep
their promise. They didn't want to go to church in their
jeans, but she assured them that they were dressed fine.
The pastor gave an altar call at the end of the sermon,
and when he asked those who had raised their hands
to come forward, they both stepped out surprised to
see the other going forward. They accepted Christ that
day. My parents agreed that our time of crisis was a
small price to pay for the salvation of two loved ones.

After thirteen days in the intensive care unit, Dad
was put on a regular floor where they hooked him up
to multiple machines. Soon he was ready to see results
of yet another miracle, and so were we. He pleaded,
"God, if what I believe is true—that you spared my
life on three separate occasions (once from the stroke,
once from almost hemorrhaging to death at home, and
once from my surgery when I went into complete body

failure)—then I don't believe you would have me die of a virus that wasn't my fault."

Deep within his heart, Dad believed God was going to do something big; at times we all wondered if God might say, "No." Nurses walked in with gloves on their hands for protection, and Dad didn't know if he should kiss my mom or even hug us kids because of this virus. But he threw off all the doubt that entangled him and he believed!

My dad asked the doctors to test his blood again, but the doctor's replied, "Evan, there's no mistake. When you've got it, you've got it."

But Dad was relentless and persisted, and five tests were again administered and sent to three major laboratories. After several days, the doctors hadn't given us any word, so Dad asked, "Doctor, do we have any results yet?"

"Yes, one set has come back."

"It's negative, isn't it?"

With hesitation and very little eye contact, he said, "Yes, it is." But he continued to remind us that we really needed to face reality and that the other tests would confirm our fears. During the next two weeks, all the tests came back: *Negative!*

Some people would say, "He must never have had the AIDS virus in the first place," but that's not what the doctors told us: "When you've got it, you've got it." And my dad would say with the goofiest grin, "Doctor, when you're healed, you're healed."

Another confirmation came about some time later when dad was preaching and sharing his testimony in a nearby town of Jefferson City and a young woman approached him. She told him that she was one of the nurses who had been caring for him at the hospital. When they put a scope down his esophagus to investigate the complexity of his situation, they found the fungus that is often evident in those who are carriers of the HIV virus. She said her and the doctors immediately knew that he was carrying this virus. That is, in fact, how they initially knew and then confirmed by blood tests. She praised God with us that he was free and clear of the HIV virus.

> Ask, and it will be given to you; seek, and you will find; knock, and it will be opened to you. For everyone who asks receives, and he who seeks finds, and to him who knocks it will be opened.
>
> *Matthew 7:7–8 (NAS)*

My God could do anything. I was sold! He was the greatest. God was officially my hero! How could I ever doubt Him again?

MY KINGDOM

Heather

High school took its toll on me. My walk-on-water faith began sinking as I began to lose sight of God's power. I began to lose sight of God all together as my little world started to unravel. New family crises left me groping for air as I worked extra hard to keep my head above the rising water. The Lord had built a powerful testimony for my family; as a result, the enemy put a rather large target on our backs. Never before had we faced such opposition. My family was falling apart before my eyes.

Even though God saved my dad's life physically, he still battled daily health issues. He was doing amazingly well in spite of the doctors' predictions, but his physical issues wore on him emotionally and spiritually. In the past my father had struggled with a short temper, and now his frustration with his new inabilities brought his anger to a head once again. He was letting God work on his anger, but some days his outbursts wounded us as a family.

My mom also struggled. She was exhausted from being so strong while Dad was in the hospital that she didn't find comfort in the Lord; instead she found comfort in the arms of our manipulative pastor who was also her boss. Their hidden relationship escalated and continued for a year before it was brought to light. During that year, this pastor belittled my father as a man, a pastor, a husband, and a father to my mother and others in the church. When the truth was revealed, our family was nearly destroyed. Mom and Dad both lost their jobs, and almost overnight my church family was taken away from me.

All the stability I had was suddenly gone, as was everything that was good and pure in my life. I tried to comprehend with my sixteen-year-old mind what it meant to have an affair. And I tried to understand how a man could stand before me every Sunday and lead so many to the cross and then call my mother—or any of the other women in the congregation whom he preyed upon—for a rendezvous that very night.

I wanted to hate my mom for her actions, but her tears told me she was sorry, and I had to forgive her. I wanted to understand my father's pain, but I couldn't see past his exploding anger and rage. I didn't fully comprehend the scars the affair left on his heart until I was married and could fathom the rejection and torture it must have incurred.

God wanted to be my escape in those rising waters, but I was scared. My understanding of church and God had merged together, and everything I once knew the church to be had become a show and a lie. I was hurting, and the church didn't care. I was shunned, and the church closed its doors on me. As a result, I thought God didn't care and that He was turning his back on me; and who wants to hand over control to a God like that? Surely I could find something secure and good that would comfort the ache in my heart.

Did you ever read the "Choose Your Own Adventure" books as a child? I loved them because they always gave me a choice. If I thought Choice A would end how I wanted, I picked Choice A. But if I didn't like that outcome, I simply read the book again and picked Choice B. There's nothing like a big do-over, and that's what I wanted, so I began making my own choices. That meant thinking twice before picking Choice A, especially in light of what was happening in my family and what I wanted for my life. I gradually shifted my focus from Christ to myself and started building my own kingdom. My kingdom had less rules and more freedom, and I enjoyed the comfy throne. I didn't ask God to pack His bags completely because sometimes I had need of Him. I still believed in Him, but I didn't believe that His plans were the absolute best. I had plans of my own—good plans—and these plans included bringing Him into my kingdom when I needed His help.

By the time I left for college, I had warped God-Hero of my childhood into God-Servant, who was at my beck and call, wrapped around my little finger. And that's where I planned to keep Him. I believed He and the world revolved around me and that He would do whatever I asked because *I* wanted it done. When I was in trouble, I lit up my God signal just like the citizens of Gotham City powered up the bat signal when they needed Batman.

Like most college students, I was ready to brave the wild and make my dreams a reality. With my to-do list clutched tightly in hand, I set off for Southwest Baptist University and began my quest. My plan was simple: get a degree, meet some incredible friends, be involved, meet the man of my dreams, fall in love, get married, have some children, and live in a cute house with a white picket fence. After all, no real list is complete without the fence. We didn't need to be rich; I just wanted enough to go shopping every once in a while. It was the perfect plan for building the perfect kingdom.

College was almost too good to be true. I found myself checking items off my list left and right. I was right where I wanted: enjoying my classes, doing well in my major, making friends, and surviving on my own.

I met so many people with backgrounds similar to mine, and connecting with them was easy. In fact, I almost had too many good friends to choose from. But as I made new friends, something unexpected happened. I felt a gnawing in my spirit. God was drawing me to Him—pursuing me through my friends. I saw a real relationship with God that I was missing in my relationship with Him. They had a kind of friendship with Him that made me thirsty.

"There's more," He whispered. "Come and drink."

The more I witnessed their love of God, the more I saw my lack of love for Him. They talked to Him and about Him and made decisions based on what He wanted. Their love for Him propelled them to give themselves away, and they did so through campus ministries and in their churches. And I thought *I* had discovered their secret, but *God* was calling me—inviting me to truly find Him. Until then I wasn't aware I was standing in a desert—I was dry and parched and in need of the living water He was offering. I wanted to know Him, to love Him, and be healed by Him, for His beckoning was clear, and I saw the oasis of more before me. I glanced at my list and noticed "more" wasn't there. It should've been, so I quickly added it.

God became another object to obtain—another box to check off my list. He had other plans. He didn't want to be *on* my list, He wanted to *be* my list. My kingdom kept me from experiencing all He had for me in His kingdom, and we battled for control of my heart. I fought so hard against giving all. All? I was quite confident I could only give some. He was asking me to step into His kingdom, but I first had to surrender my kingdom. But mine was so safe. Predictable. I was building my kingdom with *my* list, *my* wants, *my* hopes, *my* dreams, *my* ideas, and *my* God.

When I was a child, I used to speak like a child,
think like a child, reason like a child.

1 Corinthians 13:11 (NAS)

As children, one of the first words we learn is *mine,* and it
was hard to deprogram myself from that state of mind. I
rationalized that God wanted me to have my kingdom—
that He wanted me to live a happy, fulfilled life.

Though I struggled, I let God begin working in
me. My hunger for Scripture increased, I spent more
time talking to Him, I began singing in a girls' vocal
group. My arm was about to break from the hours of
patting myself on the back. Everything was going as
planned and was actually better than I'd imagined. I
had verbally surrendered, but my list was still tucked
away in my pocket.

And then I met James. Introduced at a bonfire, I
was immediately drawn to his smile. He was silly without being stupid, daring without being reckless, and
smart without being boring. I felt a slight tug on my
heartstrings, but I quickly reminded myself that I had
just ended a two-year relationship and wasn't ready for
another one. Besides, he was a year younger than me
and that was a good enough reason to ignore the feelings stirring in my heart.

Months later I met a friend for lunch, and she saw
James in the parking lot and invited him to join us
without asking me. Blimpie's sandwiches never tasted
so good. We shared a table by the window and laughed
and talked and laughed some more, and I was again
reminded of what I felt when I first laid eyes on him.
Something about him made me want to know more.

I left that day with a little spring in my step. I must bump into this boy again! And I guess his plan was to bump into me as well. I saw him everywhere: lunch, my dorm, the Student Union. In an instant we were inseparable. Normal days were no longer ordinary but were full of life and adventure. Even if it hadn't been springtime, everything still would have looked new and alive through my new rose-colored glasses.

James was unlike anyone I had ever met. He lived freely and wasn't tied to a list. He flew by the seat of his pants and would block out intimidating voices that said, "You shouldn't," or "You can't." He'd say, "Watch me!" To top off his sense for adventure, he was good at everything. He was heavily involved with theatre and loved to act on or off stage, and he could imitate whatever character he could think of. He would make me laugh so hard I'd cry. My aching sides made me think about limiting my time with him but nothing seemed reason enough to be where he was not.

More than the laughing and the adventures, he radiated a deep love for his God. James cherished his King, and this genuine adoration made me want more of God again. In all he did and every decision he made, James sought to please the Lord and was determined to surrender his life as he served his master. Confidence exuded from every part of his being, for James lived by the rules of Christ's kingdom. James was a servant, and when God called him, he'd go—no questions asked.

We began dating in April my sophomore year and spent most of our free time together. When we didn't have free time, we made free time. Soon the days turned into months, and we still couldn't get enough of each other. Our hearts had become vulnerable in each other's hands. Before either of us could blink to break our lovey-dovey gaze, summer was here. As we packed our college rooms to go to our respective homes for the summer, we vowed to spend as much time together as possible. Summer break didn't seem like a break at all, not with long phone calls, surprise visits, and tearful departures.

One weekend his family invited me to visit, and James had a surprise for me. He took me to his church, and as we sat at the piano, he sang a song over me—a song to my heart. Within the song, he confessed his love for me. *Love*—a word he had saved for the one he believed God had for him. My heart was his, and his was mine.

Within the next year, we would once again sit on the stage of his church as he proposed to me. After I said, "Yes!" through muffled tears of joy, we committed our relationship and engagement to the Lord. We knelt at the altar and asked God to bless our relationship and our future together.

The very next year, in the same room, on the same stage, we professed our love to one another before our family, our friends, and our God, and vowed to live for better or for worse, in sickness and in health, 'til death do us part. Or as I liked to call it, forever to whatever.

> For this reason a man shall leave his father and mother, and be joined to his wife; and they shall become one flesh.
>
> *Genesis 2:24 (NAS)*

We were one. I glanced at my list again and smiled. God was making all my dreams come true! He *was* my hero. I couldn't understand how anyone could question God's love; His gifts were perfect and more wonderful than I could have dreamed. God was safe, near, and loving. He was my gift giver.

HOLLY'S KINGDOM

Holly

In theory, our family should've been stronger than ever after my dad's miraculous healing. We were riding high on the wings of God's grace and mercy, but after a while, things began to unravel. Though the Lord had healed my dad, he was still walking with a walker and constantly choking on food. He had been quick to get upset with us before his stroke, but now Dad would ignite with greater anger more quickly than before. I didn't fully understand this until later, but Dad was depressed from his frustrations with his health and with his work at the church. We all walked on eggshells while in his presence, and I began looking for a way to get out of the house.

I was sixteen, and I used my car keys as a means to escape when things were unpleasant. A new relationship also took my mind off the difficulties of home, and though it started innocently, I was soon into something over my head and was dating a man nine years older. Even though I was uncertain about the boundaries I was nearing, I didn't reach out for help, and I was not willing to admit to myself that I was trapped. I felt so lost.

Meanwhile, Dad was back in the hospital, and Mom was holding the house together while spending every extra moment she had with Dad and balancing a new baby at home. She had so much on her plate.

> He rescues them from death … We put our hope in the LORD.
>
> He is our help and our shield.
>
> In Him our hearts rejoice, for we trust in His holy name.
>
> *Psalm 33:19–21 (NLT)*

I wish I had confided in someone sooner about the relationship that I was in that was spinning out of control, but because I didn't fully understand what was happening, I didn't. (Even as I write this, my heart aches, but I thank God that He doesn't give up on us.) Eventually I reached out for help and confided in my pastor, who prayed with me and encouraged me to talk to my parents. I knew talking to him would be hard, but I knew it was the right thing to do. I'll never forget the

Scripture that my pastor prayed over me that night: "So now there is no condemnation for those who belong to Christ Jesus" (Romans 8:1 NLT).

What joy filled my heart! The ugly weight of sin in my life I carried no more! I began to shed my mistakes from that relationship and began the journey of restoration and healing in my beautiful God. He was making my path straight once again. All that was rough and jagged, He began to smooth.

I made it out of that dark place, but recovery took time. My dad was merciful at first, but he struggled with resentment and trust issues that manifested themselves with anger; he was angry about the pain and wounds that I had and would carry, angry that now he found himself with new feelings of distrust for his own daughter, and angry that he couldn't turn back the clock and do things differently. Just when I thought we were moving forward, he would lash out at me. I understand now that his own circumstances and inadequacies, compounded with his illness, caused him to sometimes react in such harsh ways.

Even though I struggled to gain my dad's approval, for my own healing I had to deal with my heavenly Father. He had started a work in my heart, but I didn't feel instantly close to Him—it was like getting reacquainted with a good friend. He never made me feel distant, but because I couldn't forgive my own sin, I felt far away from His presence. Even so, the Lord sweetly and tenderly called to me despite my blemishes and mistakes.

My heart has heard You say, "Come and talk with
me."

   And my heart responds, "Lord, I am coming."

Psalm 27:8 (NLT)

I began to learn that we can't be hesitant when we seek
God. We need to run to Him when our heart is heavy,
and we need to cling to Him when the darkness seems
endless. Scripture declares, "So let us come boldly to
the throne of our gracious God. There we will receive
His mercy, and we will find grace to help us when we
need it most" (Hebrews 4:16 NLT).

My senior year was almost more than I could bear.
Dad wrestled with his feelings toward Mom following
the affair, and the police came to our house on several occasions because we thought Dad might seriously
hurt her or one of us kids. The school year drew to a
close, and unlike most high school graduates, I had no
idea where I was going or what I wanted to do. I only
knew I was ready to leave home.

One night that summer, I lay in bed praying about
escaping my never-ending turmoil, and I began thinking about college. Dad had always tried to persuade me
to go to Moody Bible Institute in Chicago, and there
were two very appealing things about this school: 1) it
was far away from home, and 2) it was a Christian Bible
college.

I immediately applied to MBI and was wait-listed,
but one week before orientation, Moody called with
an opening for me. I was thrilled! I was ready for the
energy of the city, the sound of the el train, and an

escape from the yelling and screaming that so often surrounded me. But as I was packing, my heart became anxious with fear. Could my sisters and brother survive home without me? When things got rough, I was often the buffer between them and the severity of the situation. I knew the Lord would take care of them, so I left for Chicago in August 1993 to begin my freshman year of college.

It was time to dream! I had always loved music and had always wanted to be in full-time ministry. My love for music began when I was a child; my mother often sang in the car and harmonized with the lead singer on the radio, and the rest of us would sing along with her. But it wasn't only music that I loved—I loved singing praise to Jesus in worship to Him. At the same time, despite my family's failures and hiccups, I also had a heart for ministry—for loving the Lord and loving people—that my parents had instilled in me from childhood. Dad often took me with him when he visited people in the hospital or nursing homes, and he let me sing to the sweet ladies who were weathered from life as he prayed with those who were desperate for a miracle.

> Don't just pretend that you love others. Really love them. Hate what is wrong. Stand on the side of good. Love each other with genuine affection, and take delight in honoring each other. Never be lazy in your work, but serve the Lord enthusiastically.
>
> *Romans 12:9–11 (NLT)*

I arrived at MBI in August of 1993, ready for my new-found freedom. I'd love to say that I was eager to dive into my studies but that was not the case. My eyes were set on the social scene. Shortly after school started I met some musicians who enjoyed writing music and performing together, and they invited me to join them. We called ourselves Thomas's Wanderings and practiced or recorded almost every night. Within the next few months we opened for Steve Camp, Michael Card, and Sixpence None the Richer at area concerts.

One night that fall some girls from my dorm invited me to join them and their brother floor for dinner, and since I didn't have any plans, I agreed to go. As the group assembled in the foyer of the girl's dorm, a tall guy wearing a California Angels hat caught my attention. The way he leaned against the wall suggested that he might be a little more reserved than the rest of the guys, and I thought, "He is one of the most beautiful men I have ever seen."

Our group proceeded on foot to our destination, and I trailed behind just a bit. As we approached busier streets and a darker park, the "beautiful one" joined me, for he was purposefully walking behind the group to make sure we were all safe. We made conversation until we arrived at The West Egg, where we ended up sitting across from each other. He ordered buffalo wings, and I learned that he grew up near Buffalo, New York. He talked a lot about his family, explaining that he was the youngest of nine and that he came from a family of apple farmers. He grew up on a large apple orchard nestled right on Lake Ontario, and many of his family members still lived there. It sounded too good to be true; his family seemed picture perfect and very stable, and I was taken with him from the beginning.

When I returned to my dorm room that night, I told some girls about the amazing guy I had met from Buffalo, and it so happened that one of them was from that area and needed a ride home for Thanksgiving. What a perfect reason to call him—that night! (Patience has never been my strong suit.) I could tell he was surprised when he heard my voice, but he said he was happy that I called because he was, in fact, getting ready to call me to see if I was interested in going to church with him and his roommates that Sunday.

After attending church with Scott and his friends, he later called and asked me out on an official date. I couldn't believe it! I honestly thought he was way out of my league; he was a talented soccer player for MBI and an upperclassman. Some of my friends were in shock about this development and told me that many girls had tried to catch his attention in the past year. He never seemed to notice or look their way and was always focused and untouchable.

For our first date Scott took me to see *Joseph and the Amazing Technicolor Dream Coat*. This was my first Broadway-type musical, and I was dreadfully nervous but had a wonderful time. Afterward we walked back to campus and stopped for dessert. Things were definitely looking up.

As Scott and I grew closer, I shared with him what my family had been going through. He had a sympathetic ear and comforted me in such a sweet and tender way, and he opened my eyes to why my dad had reacted the way he did. Of course, Scott didn't condone my dad's violent outbursts, but he helped me see how this act of betrayal—compounding with his physical condition—affected his marriage, children, work, ministry, church, and friendships. Shortly after that conversation, I called my dad and told him that I better understood what he was going through. I forgave him for his outbursts of violence, and we had a real breakthrough in our relationship.

At home my family was mending too, and God began to heal my mom and dad's marriage. During my second semester of school, Dad called and woke me up early one Saturday morning. "Holly, your mom and I have something we need to tell you."

He handed the phone over to my mom, who said, "Boy, I could sure use some pickles and ice cream right now." They were having another baby! And they were so happy! I knew this baby was part of how God was restoring their marriage and life, but I had mixed emotions about a new member of our family. For starters, I was almost twenty years old. Even so, I was really excited for them. I knew this pregnancy wasn't the "answer" to their marital woes, but this baby became a new symbol of God's restoration in their lives.

MY ROCK & SCOTT'S DREAM

It didn't happen immediately, but Scott soon became my rock, and I started going to him first for wisdom rather than God. Before I knew it, he began to replace God as my first source of strength, and my dependence on God declined over time.

The end of my first year at Moody drew to a close, and one night we were on the phone discussing where we saw ourselves in the distant future. He shared with me his dream to start a Christian adventure camp for troubled teens and inner-city youth, and I shared my desire to be involved in some sort of Christian music career. I know we both wondered if we would be able to blend those dreams together.

I traveled overseas with the Moody Chorale for their summer mission trip, and when I returned, it was evident that I would not be able to return to Moody for the fall semester. I didn't have the money, and Mom and Dad were doing everything they could to keep their heads financially above water. Even so, I was not about to leave Chicago, Scott, or the band. Dad was not pleased with my decision to drop out of school and stay in the city, but I found an apartment and a job, and Thomas's Wanderings had gigs almost every weekend. Scott began his final year at Moody, and he also worked as a ball boy for the Chicago Bulls during Michael Jordan's reign. He always left me will call tickets for the games. His friends thought this was a waste, but I can assure you that it was not. I watched Scott every second of those games.

My desire to pursue my musical career increased, but Scott's desire to be with me if I remained in music decreased. More than once he told me that a life on the road was not how he wanted to live his life; he wanted something simple and steady. At lunch one day he proceeded to give me an ultimatum: "Holly, you need to choose what you want. It's me or music." What a dagger to my heart! Oh, how I desperately wanted both. I loved Scott but singing was all I had ever wanted to do. After much prayer and deliberation, I chose him, and I packed my bags and moved home to Missouri, hoping for a proposal in my near future.

In Missouri I found a job to pass the time and spent hours on the phone with Scott. We rarely got to see each other, but finally I was able to catch a flight to New York. I was beyond excited. We had been dating two years, and my friends and family had started pressuring me about my marital future. I knew for sure that Scott would propose on this trip.

Soon after arriving in New York, though, I knew I would not hear, "Holly, will you marry me?" But I couldn't return to Missouri without a ring on my finger, so I began applying a little pressure—okay, lots of pressure. We started looking at rings, and he did indeed propose the last night of my stay. I later found out that I made Scott feel so bad that he asked his brother, whom he worked for at the time, for an advance so he could buy an engagement ring. When I learned this, I felt awful. I know I didn't force him to ask me, but I wish

I had been more patient. Even so, he was sweet to put up with me like that.

We departed with another tearful goodbye at the airport, but I was comforted knowing that soon we would be together—forever. While in Missouri, I often questioned whether I was right in giving up my singing ambitions. At one point I almost called off the engagement, but I loved Scott so much, and I wanted to do whatever he asked. I took peace in remembering something Dad once told me: "If God has truly given your gift to you, He will provide a way for you to use it."

On March 30, 1996, Philip Scott Nesbitt and I, Holly Ann Wall, were joined in marriage. What a beautiful day! We were so happy. After opening our gifts at my parent's home, Scott and I loaded up our Jeep Cherokee and headed for New England to honeymoon at several bed and breakfast spots throughout New York and New Hampshire.

After our honeymoon we settled into our new home next to Scott's mom and dad at the apple orchard. Our house was a little run down, but it was in a beautiful spot. We could hear the waves of Lake Ontario crash against the rocks at night while we lay in bed, and the smell of the apple blossoms was heavenly. Scott's family ushered me into their close-knit family, and his mom and sister Julie, became my dear companions. My love and admiration for them grew every day.

Spring was in the air on the farm and that meant that Scott's duties kicked into overdrive. He worked around the clock, morning and night, which was a major adjustment for me. I was not accustomed to the hard work that accompanied farm life, and I did not weather it very well. I was lonely and took my frustration out on my poor husband who I'm sure just wanted some peace and quiet when he walked through the door. I made him and myself miserable because I didn't know what to do with myself all day. Everyone seemed to have a routine that they gladly followed, but I was struggling to find my place. I remember Scott asked me, "What happened to the woman I fell in love with?" I responded, "I don't know."

We both agreed that I needed something to keep me busy, so I found a job in Rochester, New York. During the forty-five-minute drive to and from work, I saturated myself with biblical teachings from David Jeremiah and Joyce Meyer. They rejuvenated me and uplifted my spirit, and I began praying for God to open doors for me to witness for Him—which He did—and my faith continued to grow. For the first time in a while, I felt like myself again, and Scott noticed the change too. We were finally enjoying each other's company again and valuing what each was contributing to the household.

We had been married a year and a half when we found out we were pregnant. We both hoped for a little girl, and in a conversation after church one Sunday, I said to Scott, "Whatever the gender of this baby, I pray this child looks just like you."

"Why is that?"

"Because if something ever happened to you, it would be as if I still had you with me." He shot me a weird look, and we both laughed it off, not yet knowing why God had placed such a prayer in my heart.

Early in the pregnancy, we visited Scott's brother, Mark, and his wife, Becky, in Chicago, and the four of us spent much of our time laughing together, for the boys were extremely close and shared a special connection. Near the end of our trip, we trekked to downtown Chicago to visit our good friend Charles whom we had met a few years earlier. Charles was a retired corporate executive of a well-known food chain and a good friend of Scott's sister Julie, and he often joined the family for special gatherings or when he wanted to get away from the city. We cherished his sincere friendship. While catching up with him in his home, he began asking us questions.

Charles asked Scott about his ultimate dream. If he could do anything or go anywhere, what would he do? Scott answered him by describing his vision of an adventure camp for troubled teens. Charles listened intently, nodding and encouraging us along in conversation with his smile. After Scott finished, Charles said he wanted to make our dream a reality.

We were both full of shock and numbness following that meeting. My mind kept recalling the dream Scott had shared with me years earlier while we were in school. I could hardly believe that God was acting so quickly; Scott and I honestly hadn't thought it was possible until we retired. God reminded me of His promise in Jeremiah 29:11: "'For I know the plans I have for you,' says the Lord. 'They are plans for good and not for disaster, to give you a future and a hope.'"

The three of us started planning immediately and soon we were traveling with Charles and scoping out properties in the Adirondacks and New England. We needed a place that could serve as our base camp and that had separate homes for Charles and for our family. We toured many beautiful locations, but the time we spent with Charles was most precious to me, as the three of us dreamed of what our camp could be.

Finally we found the perfect property. Nestled in Maple Corner, Vermont, with views of the Green Mountains on one side and the Adirondacks on the other were 220 beautiful acres complete with one large New England-style home, one modest Cape home with dormers, and a 30,000 square-foot red barn. But nothing compared to the land. It was stunning with a quaint pond toward the rear of the property, wide walking trails through the woods, and plenty of pasture for horses. Picture perfect.

Charles soon made an offer on the property, and once it was accepted, we began researching Vermont's requirements for a not-for-profit camp and started organizing accordingly. Scott was fascinating to watch during this time; he pulled everything together as if he had been doing it for years. I was immensely proud of him for undertaking these new challenges.

Emma Joy was born on July 6, 1998. She was precious. When he held her in his arms, Scott beamed with pride; he absolutely and completely adored her. Once we were home and began adjusting to parenthood, I quit my job to be a stay-at-home mom and to aid Scott in camp preparations. We still lived next to Scott's family, and I was thankful to have his mom close by. She helped me with the grocery shopping, meals, and laundry and offered priceless treasures of basic childcare advice. Emma was a bright spot in all of our lives, and she looked like Scott with her fine blonde hair, big blue eyes, and cute little nose that matched Scott's perfectly.

Early the next spring, we moved to Vermont. Scott's oldest sister, Cindy, and her family joined us while her husband, Tom, helped with construction around the property. They embraced Emma and loved her as if she was their own, and we loved having them with us as we embarked on this new journey.

There was much to do. More paths needed to be cleared in the woods, and the enormous barn needed to be renovated. At the same time, we needed to build our clientele, raise funds, and legalize our new organization. None of this was easy. The people of Maple Corner were wary of having inner-city youth and troubled teens in their little community. This began the hardest season in our ministry to date, but Scott kept his head up and worked harder than anyone I had ever known.

A SHAKY KINGDOM

Heather

Could my life be any sweeter? Could my days be filled with more beauty? Had I stepped into a portrait of peace and prosperity painted only with the Father's fine strokes? Was there anything He couldn't do? My heart sang, my lips praised, and my eyes welled up with thankfulness. As I marveled at my kingdom, I thought, "This is good. This is perfect."

Little did I know that soon my life would change forever.

Holly

In the fall of '99, my family came to visit Scott and I in Vermont. Though Dad wasn't feeling very well when they left Missouri, they came anyway. He figured he had a little stomach bug; but as their visit continued, Dad's health quickly deteriorated, and we soon had to take him to the hospital, where they found a complexity of issues with his body.

After a week or so in the hospital, Dad demanded to be released, but he was so sick he couldn't walk. He couldn't even stand on his own, but he was adamant about returning home to Missouri. The next day we booked flights for the entire family to return home, and I decided to go too, so I could help take care of him when Mom went back to work.

Taking care of Dad was difficult for all of us, but we had seen Dad sick like this so many times before that it really didn't faze us. Emma and I stayed with Dad while the hospital set up daily in-home health care. Days after arriving home, our nurse detected pneumonia in his lungs, and they admitted him to the hospital. This was the last place he wanted to be.

Heather

My sister Heidi called to tell me that Dad had been admitted to a hospital in Vermont but now he was home and being readmitted to the hospital in Jefferson

City. The call didn't shake me. I thought to myself, *This feels familiar.* When his body tired out, he'd return to the hospital for a while, but he always bounced back.

Because my grandparents were celebrating their fiftieth wedding anniversary, James and I were headed home anyway, but we headed for the hospital as soon as we arrived. Dad was in the intensive care unit, which meant he was in critical condition, but I was oblivious. Dad would rebound—he always did. We all loved on him and whispered in his ear that we couldn't wait for him to come home, but something in his eyes was different from his other hospital stays. Dad had been adamant about not coming to this particular hospital, which had upset my mom because she felt there was no other option. Though he connected this hospital with a lot of hard memories, the alternative was another hospital thirty-five minutes way. Mom was confident that for now this was the best place for him. And I knew God was on our side no matter where Dad was.

Once the entire family arrived, Dad's doctor pulled us aside to discuss Dad's condition. He didn't beat around the bush. "Evan is near death. His body is shutting down, and his blood is turning septic. There is little hope, and we don't expect him to make it through the night."

This news would have broken most families, but it didn't even shake us. For a moment I thought, *Could this be?* But faith quickly made doubt take a back seat, and it never surfaced again. In my heart of hearts, I knew he would beat the odds. He would once again walk out of this hospital as a walking miracle—a testimony of God's powerful healing. My God was my hero, and He could do anything. I believed a doctor's prognosis was no match for my God.

Holly

I went to Dad's room alone and began to sing some of his favorite songs. I sang "His Eye is on the Sparrow" and his favorite "He's Been Faithful" by the Brooklyn Tabernacle Choir.[3]

> *"In my moments of fear, through ev'ry pain ev'ry tear*
> *There's a God who's been faithful to me*
> *When my strength was all gone,*
> *when my heart had no song*
> *Still in love, He's proved faithful to me*
> *Ev'ry word He's promised is true*
> *What I thought was impossible, I see my God do*
> *He's been faithful, faithful to me*
> *Looking back His love and mercy, I see*
> *Though in my heart I have ques-*
> *tioned, even failed to believe*
> *Yet He's been faithful, faithful to me."*

I just let my heart sing that afternoon as he lay there lifeless in that hospital room. I saw no movement, no response indicating that he could hear, but I felt that I should do it. Suddenly several nurses and a doctor came quickly into the room and asked what I was doing. I told them that I was singing to him, and they said I must continue because his blood pressure and heart rate had stabilized in the time that I had been in there! I drew closer to his body and prayed to God that he could hear me. I sang through my tears as my heart cried, "Lord, show Yourself faithful once again."

We lifted our voices to God and thanked Him in advance for the healing that would bring about Dad's recovery. Just as before, we sat in the waiting room, and the same people came to encourage us, the same people came to pray with us, and the same people came believing.

At home, we crawled into bed, saying, "Tomorrow we're going to see the glory of God." Mom stayed at the hospital with Dad, and it occurred to me that I should stay out of kindness to her, but I decided to be strong for my younger siblings and stay at home. My youngest sister Hannah, who was just nine-years-old, was shaken by the situation, so she and I prayed together to comfort her worried heart. I slept with her that night, and before we turned out the light, I said, "It will be better tomorrow. You'll see."

> And the prayer offered in faith will restore the one who is sick, and the LORD will raise him up.
>
> *James 5:15 (NAS)*

The ringing phone pierced the silence of the house. I sprang out of bed disoriented, but fear gripped my heart as I woke up. I knew Mom was calling. Was something wrong? Holly and I answered at the same time and heard my mom's quivering voice on the other end. "Your dad passed away a few minutes ago. He's with the Lord."

"No. No! That's not possible!" I said. I tried to muffle my cries so I wouldn't awake the little ones.

From across the hall and through the phone receiver, I could hear Holly. "What," she said. "What?"

"It all happened so fast. I was in the waiting room and heard 'code blue' over the intercom, and I knew it was your dad." We sat on the line and sobbed with one another. "I'll be home as soon as I can to tell the others," Mom said.

Holly and I ran out of our rooms and hugged for a second but there was no comfort in our embrace. I ran down the hall and headed for downstairs to find James. He had heard the phone ring and was headed upstairs. As he rounded the corner and stood at the bottom of the stairs, our eyes met, and I said, "He's dead!" He ran up the stairs and grabbed me and held me for the longest time. Tears fell as my heart broke into a million pieces. *Why didn't God save him this time?*

Everything stood still. As we waited for Mom to come home, I had flashbacks of my dad in the hospital—the last time I was to be with him on this earth. Flashbacks of the phone ringing, of Hannah's eyes that were full of fear just hours ago, and my prayer of belief that today he'd come home. *He is home.* But that's not what I meant! I hadn't prayed for God to take him away from us! My mind raced from thought to thought, but my body felt numb, weak, and broken. We sat in the living room, praying the kids would not wake up before Mom got home. What would we say? How would we say it? *They are so young, God, how could you let their daddy be taken from them?* Nothing made sense. Where was my hero? Why hadn't He come to our rescue this time? Did we use up all of our prayers? Were we no longer important to Him? Had we done something wrong? Was He punishing us?

When Mom finally came home, we sat as a family in the living room and held one another while we sobbed. For the first time, we had truly lost. During the next few days, people came and went, piling food on our countertops. Everything remained a blur, and in my heart, emptiness consumed me. Nothing mattered anymore.

We had one another, but it didn't seem like enough. Scott comforted Holly, James wiped away my tears, Jacob held Heidi's hand, and Mom cradled the kids. But it wasn't enough. I was tired of fighting with my thoughts and my what-ifs and the silence, yet out of love for my family, I knew we must encourage one another. I knew we must honor our father for the life he lived. We gathered all the pictures of Dad, and as we did, we laughed, wept, and remembered through each one. We made a collage of our favorite photographs for his funeral as a memorial to him.

But then came the hard part: selecting a casket. *Who cares?* I thought. I hated planning where we would lay his lifeless body, while we sat in that small room. How surreal. How disgusting. How hopeless.

His funeral service was amazing as we honored him and honored God through him. We sat with others who had witnessed something different in him and celebrated a servant who was finally home. *Home*—that sweet word that kept him going through the long days in the hospital. God had been anxiously waiting to bring him home to a place that rescued him from the struggles of his torn, earthly body. In heaven he wasn't fighting his failing body parts; he had complete healing. We pictured him dancing, running, laughing, and playing golf—doing all the things that had been impossible for him for the last nine years. We celebrated his love for God, his family, and the church, and we remembered him as a minister to ministers. We left confident that we had cherished him in our hearts, and peace walked us out of church that day. Even through our tears, smiles emerged, as we were confident that we would see him again.

But in the quiet, I could not make sense of it all. I wept in the dark, grieving over the loss. The more and more I thought about it, the more hardened my heart became. *Why did this happen?* I had been so happy and so content in the life that God had given me. God was not being fair!

> I'm not letting up—I'm standing my ground. My complaint is legitimate.
>
> God has no right to treat me like this—it isn't fair!
>
> *Job 23:1–5 (MSG)*

My kingdom had been so safe and peaceful, but in one moment—one fell swoop—a wrecking ball flew into my castle and threw me off my throne and onto the cold ground. As I searched for my crown, which had been whisked off in all the commotion, the floor beneath me shook as an earthquake tore through the land. I knew I had lost control. Or did I ever have control to begin with?

> He has stripped me of my honor and removed the crown from my head.
>
> *Job 19:9 (NIV)*

One moment I was in control of everything, but seconds later it became clear that I hadn't a thing in my possession. My arms flailed to grasp anything that could hold me steady, and there He was. He was calling me to hold onto Him. "I have torn you, but I will heal you. I have wounded you, but I will bandage you. My child, come into My kingdom."

But I turned away from His outstretched arm. My heart said, "Who are you? My Savior or my destroyer? You can't be trusted! I don't know who *You* are anymore. I thought You were *for* me. Now I see that You're against me!" I refused to take His hand that day. *I* would find peace and comfort and all that had been robbed from me. The earthquakes still resonated through the hills, and the destruction was evident as I scanned my once beautiful palace. I had built it once, and I knew I could build it again. My life was not over, and I would rebuild that which had been ruined. My kingdom would be saved!

> For whoever wishes to save his life will lose it, but whoever loses his life for My sake, he is the one who will save it.
>
> *Luke 9:24 (NAS)*

It was easy to say the right things. I was surrounded by God-loving people who cared for me and wanted to make sure I was grieving properly. The Christian clichés were on every card, in every letter, and on every condoning tongue. I knew the truth, and I believed that it was the truth, but it didn't mend my broken heart. Those good words didn't make me magically better, and they didn't take root in my soul.

Part of me really wanted them to sink in, but part of me just wanted to be mad. I had a right to be mad! I was supposed to have a dad to grow old with me and a dad to hold my children in his arms as I said, "Dad, look, she has Mom's eyes and your smile." He was supposed to be there for his four-year-old son, Hunter, who would now hardly remember his dad. Heath was supposed to have a dad to go to all his basketball games and yell that the coach never played him enough. Dad was supposed to tear up when Hannah-Banana had a crush on the boy down the street. He was supposed to answer our questions when we bought a house or a car. Four-and-a-half months ago he had walked me down the aisle and given me away as a bride, and he was supposed to be here now, when I was hurting, when I was sad, and when I was confused. My dad was supposed to always be here for me! Not heaven! Not yet.

I let my rights cloud the truth. I shut my ears to His voice. I wanted to stay mad, and I thought that would show Him! But in all my scheming to teach God a lesson, my heart hurt like never before. Emptiness consumed me and deep sorrow became my best friend. Pain held my hand, as I chose to take the path of resentment instead of His path of healing. His voice echoed, "I have torn you, but I will heal you." Not this time.

Holly responded differently. Although she missed her daily daddy phone call with him on the other end of the line with his goofy voice trying to impersonate someone or a report on his last golf score, she was able to cry out for the Lord to comfort her. She would say, "When I am in God's presence, it makes me feel so much closer to Dad."

The battle continued to rage within me, but I didn't let others know how hard it was for me to even get out of bed in the morning. I wanted to wake up from this horrible nightmare and start the day over, but every morning I awoke with the reality that life was no longer right and there was no way to fix it. James was doing everything he could to comfort me; he tried to help me see that God was and had always been in control. He reminded me of when God proved His faithfulness to my family and me and asked how I could turn my fist toward Him with this first big disappointment.

"We can't understand His ways," he said. "We can only trust that He is still God and promise to follow Him no matter what." But I pushed truth away. God didn't deserve my love; His hand had crushed my trust. How can I love someone who wanted to hurt me?

During my toughest nights, James would hear me in bed crying as he stayed up late studying. He was worried about me and knew that I wasn't grieving the way God wanted me to grieve. He said, "I can hear it in the way you cry. You are crying as if you have no hope."

And when it came down to it, he was right. I didn't

have hope. Hope had left me when my hero hadn't come for me. I was on my own to fend for my own happiness.

> Come to Me, all who are weary and heavy-laden, and I will give you rest.
>
> *Matthew 11:28 (NAS)*

COMPLETE DESTRUCTION

I was tired, and there were times when God's beckoning to come sounded very inviting. It was so tangible, so real, and so full of promise that I would take a few steps in His direction with heart in hand. With each step, my arm moved forward to place my heart in His hands, but I quickly reminded myself of what He'd done to it before, and I'd snatch it back, holding it tight against my chest with both hands. I trusted Him before, but He would have to earn my trust if He wanted my heart again.

I was searching for solid ground, a place to feel safe, and someplace to feel at home, but I wasn't even at home in my own skin. *How can one event ruin me?*

In many worship services, I sat unable to sing—my mouth unable to form the words to utter a sound. I had sung to Him so many times before, but had I meant it? I couldn't say, "I surrender all." Disappointment held my mouth silent; but my tears sang for me, and they wouldn't stop singing their song of doubt and disillusionment.

Grasping for control, I filled my time by pouring more love on James. He hadn't let me down, and I believed with all my heart that he could be trusted. But no matter how hard I showered love on him, there was still an emptiness screaming inside me. We were newlyweds, so why did my heart feel so empty? It hadn't been like this before. James knew that I needed to surrender my will to the Lord, but every time I tried, I couldn't give up my rights or my control.

I had good days—days when I barely noticed the heaviness that surrounded me. I used distractions to keep me right where I was, and I indulged my time with work, family, James, television, or whatever else I could find that would take my mind away from reality. I knew the right things to say, and I knew the truth, so it was easy for me to wear a mask and say that I was fine and that I would see Dad again. In reality, the truth could not take root in my heart, so I continued to live with my mask handy.

Our family had always been close, and I believed that this mountain we faced would bring us together. I cared for them so much. I would be a help—a rescuer in times of trouble who was on call if things got too tough for my mom. Heidi lived with her husband in

Colorado, and Holly and her family lived in Vermont, but I was only about two hours from my mom and the kids, so anytime there was a hint of trouble, James and I raced home. Our role was to help and support, but I was ready to be the superhero that God was not.

Heath worried me. He was at the critical age of thirteen, and without a father figure, I wondered what would become of him. Would he stray? Could my mom handle all this on her shoulders? I wanted James to step up and hold Heath accountable and be his mentor and friend. But the distance made it hard to be the answer to our problems. I looked out for the best interest of my family, and I was determined to not let anything happen to them, but I couldn't fix our trials. I couldn't take away the pain and the loneliness that filled our home. Even in my own helplessness, I tried to convince Heath and Hannah to be strong. I felt alone in my responsibility to convince everyone to hang in there, to not give up, and to not lose heart. Confused and angry, I watched my mom struggle to find a firm place to stand. My cheerleading, although flowing from a sincere heart, may have been nothing more than a mere attempt to convince myself that if I spoke loud enough or with the right words that maybe they would believe me—maybe I would believe me. I was again helpless and left blaming God for more disappointments.

James was about to graduate, and we started thinking about our future. What was next for us? James was finishing up a double major in theater and religious studies at SBU, and he desperately desired to go on to seminary, so God could continue equipping him in knowledge and biblical truths. After applying and being accepted to Southwestern Baptist Theological Seminary (SBTS) in Fort Worth, Texas, James felt a peace that this was the next step for us.

But in the middle of this decision, we wondered what we should do with our summer. We could stay in Bolivar and prepare for our move to Dallas in August, or we could make the transition to Texas earlier, find jobs, and get settled before James started school in the fall. But we were drawn to Holly and Scott's invitation to be camp guides after they told us the vision for their Christian adventure camp, which was set to launch that summer.

We would pack all we had, store it, and spend the summer working in Vermont. It would be something different—something adventuresome—something outdoors, and I was a girlie-girl who chose pumps over hiking boots and makeup over sun block any day of the week. I reckoned I could be a little more outdoorsy and experience this other way of life. And when else would James and I have the freedom to pack up everything to be with family all summer while experiencing a place we'd never been, in a culture that we'd never seen, and doing things we'd never done? Once James got into school and then a church, we wouldn't be able to take opportunities like this.

Holly and I counted down the days until we'd be together. I couldn't even imagine the fun we might have and hoped that by being someplace new, I'd escape the heaviness that surrounded me. Surely this would help me pull it together. We packed and stored our belongings and set off for Vermont.

My heart filled with joy when we arrived at camp,

and a sense of peace that foreshadowed a promise of quieting the noise within surrounded me. The campgrounds were beautiful, and I could hardly take it all in. The hills rolled, and the mountaintops hid in majestic clouds. I vowed that I had never seen a sky so blue, clouds so full, or grass so green; God's creation was filled with new depth and wonder. But when I looked around the campground, I saw the work that was in store for us. We had much to do and very little time before the campers arrived. The barn, which had been previously used as such, was nowhere near completion. Eventually this monstrous building would hold a climbing wall, dining facility, game room, lounge, offices, and staff living quarters, but when we arrived, it was a mere skeleton of what it was supposed to be. Beyond the barn, tent sites for our guests had not been prepared, and we were not trained for our main jobs as camp guides. Campers would be arriving within weeks, and there was much to do.

Wearing the hats of camp director, construction manager, and all-around go-to guy, Scott was in high gear. He worked twenty-hour days and was in desperate need of some sleep, but sleep was not in his vocabulary. He was pressing on, and we were there to help by tackling whatever tasks were set before us, learning as we went along. The clock ticked on when our heads hit our pillows at night, and we wondered how the camp could possibly be ready for campers that summer—or even next summer! The list of unfinished tasks was longer than the list of finished tasks, but to our amazement, the barn was transformed little by little, and the

skeleton began to take shape. The first group of campers arrived a month after James and I, and as their bus
pulled in at 10:30 p.m., we were laying the last of the
floor tile in their bathrooms and making sure their
showers had running water.

While our strength stemmed from our seemingly fear-
less leader, Scott internally struggled with the pressure.

In the middle of one of our outings with the campers,
Scott and I had a chance to be alone in the car for a few
minutes. He took my hand, and with tears in his eyes,
said, "Holly, I don't know if I can continue to do this.
It's killing me. I'm so exhausted, and I can't keep doing
this to you and Emma." My heart sank to see him feel
so defeated, but I knew he was completely worn out.
The past two years had been hard, but this was the
first time I had ever heard him sound so admittedly
discouraged. Even so, I saw the light at the end of this
tunnel; several groups who had already come were giving us high marks, and youth pastors were telling us
that this was the best camp they had ever been to!

Heather

We all wanted to take a moment to prop up our feet
and catch our breath, but that required too much time,
so we took a deep breath, linked arms, and continued

on. We were supposed to be ready and excited to pour into our campers, but we were drained from the camp improvements and were mere shells of the leaders we wanted to be. I welcomed these distractions, for the war inside still raged. I kept moving and ignored any sense of the pain inside.

A few groups came and enjoyed our facility while we worked behind the scenes to complete the camp. One group signed up for a two-day canoe trip through New Hampshire, and we all set out to give them the great experience of enjoying God's beautiful creation. We were excited to do what we came here to do, but even though my title was camp guide, I felt more igno-rant and unprepared than the campers. I didn't know the first thing about roughing it or about finding the perfect place in the woods to use for a bathroom. I was lost out there, but I pressed on, following the lead of the trained individuals before me.

Things were moving at such a rapid pace. Holly desperately ached for time with her husband, for they had had family and hired help living with them five days a week for the entire year leading up to that summer.

Scott was working himself into the ground and could not come up for air, and I remember thinking, "I just have to get through this first summer. Things will slow down soon, and we can all get a break."

Scott's brother Mark worked alongside him, lightening the load when he arrived, and Scott found such relief with his presence. James and Heather were working hard, and watching Heather adjust to the rugged outdoors often made us chuckle. I could tell that this wasn't all she had dreamt it to be, but she put on a determined face, and we were just happy to be together.

It was so good to see Scott start to smile again as we got more adjusted to our first camping season. Everyone was working very hard, but seeing lives begin to change was so rewarding. I was impressed with his leadership and drive. One afternoon, a group from the newspaper—accompanied by a committee from the state capital—was scheduled to tour the property, and two hours before the appointment, Scott asked me to go buy him a new pair of jeans for the tour. I grabbed Emma and ran to Walmart, getting back minutes before the group was to arrive. Scott proudly took everyone on the tour and felt good about the question and answer time; we could tell the community was finally warming up to the idea of our camp. As Scott finished recounting to me the day's adventure, he turned to get up and walk to another room. I noticed something catching light on the back of his pants and asked him to stop. As I drew closer, I saw the long, shiny, clear sticker that manufacturers put on their clothes to indicate size. We had a good laugh about that, until his backside appeared in the newspaper later that week.

Heather

Despite my inexperience, I enjoyed the beauty that enveloped me in God's creation. Canoeing rejuvenated me after long days of cleaning and construction and allowed James and me to be together and talk. We discussed the days ahead and envisioned what we'd be doing in light of our dreams and desires. James even considered staying in the area and joining efforts with Pathway Ministries, but we both knew that seminary was his long-time dream and that we were supposed to pursue that first.

In the stillness on the water, away from the hustle and bustle of camp, the emptiness in my heart grew, and the noise in my mind and spirit increased. My heart questioned and my mind raced as I remembered easier days when everything was so full of life and peace. The summer had been hard, and though we did all we could so the Lord could use the camp, there had been road-blocks, trials, stress, lost hours of sleep, and no peace. For the past eight months, I felt that all I had known was pain—like I was always fighting an uphill battle. Where was the peace, the prosperity, and the fullness of joy? Why did everything have to be so hard?

James continued to be the voice of reason by telling me there would always be times like these. "There's going to be suffering, heartbreak, and pain, but we have to keep trusting and putting our lives in the hands of God."

One day while out on the lake, we let ourselves fall behind the other canoes, and James confronted me about the condition of my heart. "I'm worried about you. I thought you would snap out of this, but you seem to be falling deeper and deeper. I don't know what I can do to help you. I'm at a loss."

In tears, I replied that I was simply tired of fighting, that I didn't know which way was up anymore, and that I didn't want to fight these battles in my head. "Life wasn't supposed to turn out this way. God has let me down, and I don't know if I'll ever get over that."

Once the tears began, I couldn't stop them. The pain was again swallowing me whole, and I couldn't break free from the grudge I carried on my back. I was in bondage to this pain and chose to remain locked away in my castle of hopelessness. Who could save me? Could James? Could I? Could God? As the sun filled the sky and cast shimmering light across the waters, a storm raged within me. I held onto my rights and my anger, and I believed I was justified in my pain and disappointments. I could not let them go. Not yet. James continued pleading for me to trust God no matter what—even if I couldn't understand Him.

> "For My thoughts are not your thoughts, neither are your ways My ways," declares the Lord. "For as the heavens are higher than the earth, so are My ways higher than your ways and My thoughts than you thoughts."
>
> *Isaiah 55:8–9 (NAS)*

James and I took a short trip to Dallas in July to find a place to live and to iron out any remaining details before we moved there. He talked with some of his teachers, and I interviewed for a few jobs on campus.

We looked at the perfect apartment, filled out an application, and waited to hear if it was ours. As we traveled back to Vermont, we gave ourselves a pep talk, believing that we could handle a few more weeks of intense work before heading off to Texas. It took all we had to come back to camp because it had required so much of us physically that summer. It had not been at all what I had dreamed, but I still had learned a lot about myself. More than ever, I knew that I would forever be a city girl. I was ready for Dallas! Being with family had been a dream come true, and even through all the busyness and work, we had been near one another, and the time with my little two-year-old niece had been priceless.

We were excited about getting to Texas, but we needed to focus on camp for the last few weeks because there was still much to do. James and I had been asked at the beginning of the summer to find a route for a daylong canoe trip for a group of campers, which was ironic to me: I wasn't the best swimmer, and I would be helping lead the trip! James, on the other hand, was well trained in the water, had been canoeing many times, and was a lifeguard in high school.

We had searched off and on all summer, but day after day we found ourselves at a loss for a good route. Some were too short, some didn't have good places for a group to put in, and some were just too far away. The time had come to decide on a route, for the campers had already arrived on the grounds, and we were supposed to take them on their trip the next day.

James and I talked about possible routes, but I didn't know the area well enough to be confident in my suggestions. I felt so much pressure to find the right one that I petitioned for someone else to go with James. Someone who knew what to look for should go, and I was not that person. At the last minute, duties were reassigned, and Scott became available to go with James. My mind was at rest, knowing Scott was going and that he knew what he was doing.

Scott and James set off that morning to run some errands and to plan the routes they would explore that afternoon. I completed some chores around the grounds and planned to take the afternoon to write an article about my father, which a friend of mine had asked of me for an upcoming issue of *SBU Life*, SBU's alumni magazine. I had thought a great deal about the story, and James, believing this would bring about some much-needed healing for my heart, had been encouraging me to begin. I started writing that morning; but with a loss for words and heaviness all around me, I struggled with each sentence.

Around eleven thirty in the morning, James and Scott returned to camp to load the canoe and set off for the perfect route. I was so glad he had returned; I was lost and drowning and needed his help. The longer I sat there, the louder I heard the blank computer screen taunting me. James came in with a saddened look and said, "I got a speeding ticket."

I preface my response with these facts: We had no money, we were about to move to Texas, and James had a bit of a lead foot that I consistently reminded him about. Given my state of mind, this news intensified my frustration. I had wanted to be rescued from the heaviness of my moment, but instead I lashed out at him. I was relentless, blaming and pointing my finger at his failure, placing all my frustration on his shoulders. He finally just left, for there was no use in trying to talk rationally to me. That, and Scott was ready to get going.

Right before Scott headed out, he found me sitting at our kitchen table. We had had a silly argument the night before about the canoe rentals for the next day, and I'll never forget the look on his face as he quietly came and knelt by my chair and told me he was sorry for being so short with me earlier. He gave me a kiss, told me he loved me, and headed off to the vehicle to wait for James. It amazed me that he could still make my heart skip when he entered the room.

After he left, I sat and cried. Why had I been that way? Why had I been so unforgiving? Who was I turning into? I didn't like this hard person I was becoming. I wanted to pull James close—close enough so he would complete in me all that I lacked. Instead I had pushed him away with my prideful attitude and cold heart. I was exhausted and run down, so I lay down and slept.

When I awoke, no one was in the house, so I

headed off to the barn. I found most everyone in the kitchen preparing for dinner; I began helping, but my mind was elsewhere. I watched the clock, waiting for James to return so I could apologize. We never left angry. That had always been our rule, and this was exactly why: It's torture when you want to make things right and can't. The guilt builds and builds until you're about to explode! All I needed to say were four words and everything would be all-better: "I am so sorry!" Those small words magically restore relationships, heal wounds, and begin the forgiving process. I wanted to make things right more than anything.

We expected them to return around dinnertime, but they weren't back by the time dinner was served. I hoped all was going well; the pressure was on to find a good route because we were taking the group out tomorrow. As it got dark, we all wondered when they'd pull in; the darker it got, the more I longed to hear their truck coming up the road. I was about to burst with anxiousness! I wanted to be at peace with James; I wanted him to know how sorry I was and that I had been in anguish all day knowing how awful I had treated him. Every noise made me check the driveway, but there was still no sight of them. As the hours passed, we became more and more confused. Were they in need of some kind of help? Had it gotten dark too fast? Were they stuck somewhere camping over night?

Scott's brother Mark and sister Julie went looking for them. No one knew where Scott and James had gone exploring, so Mark and Julie just drove around and prayed that the Lord would lead them. They were determined not to come home without them. As they drove, they prayed, "Lord, where are they?"

The Lord replied, "Safe in the shadow of My wings," and with that, they felt a peace that James and Scott were fine. If the Lord said they were safe with Him, they could be at peace.

Holly

After Mark and Julie returned from their search, I slowly walked to our bedroom and began to pray. I asked the Lord to keep them warm through the night and bring them safely home in the morning; but as I prayed, I felt something inside of me begin to shake. A flood of emotions began to roll over me. I felt as though I were being crushed from immense pressure. I fell to my knees then to my face as I wept uncontrollably. I wasn't praying words I understood or sounds that you could comprehend. And then there were no sounds even though my lips were moving. Where was this coming from? Were they truly all right?

> As she was praying to the Lord, Eli watched her.
> Seeing her lips moving but hearing no sound…
> "I am very sad, and I was pouring my heart to the Lord. Please don't think that I am a wicked woman! For I have been praying out of great anguish and sorrow."
>
> *1 Samuel 1:12–16 (NLT)*

My heart began to break, but I could not allow it. Where was this coming from? I wiped my tears and pulled myself together. "People can't see me like this. I'm sure they're fine. Both men have outdoors and survival experience."

Before going to bed that night, I called the area hospitals to see if any accidents had been reported. No accidents with descriptions of our husbands had been reported, so I proceeded to bed with certainty that I would be awakened by my lover's face.

✒ *Heather*

Mark and Julie's word from the Lord seemed to also put Holly at peace—but not me. Those words didn't ease my mind because I was so full of fear. Holly and I prayed that God would protect them and keep them through the night, and everyone reassured us that the boys would be back by daylight with a wild story. Holly said, "I'm not worried. Scott knows so much about survival, and things like this happen. If they aren't back by daylight, then I'll be worried."

I went up to my room to try to get some sleep, and I kept the bedside lamp on, so when James returned I'd be awakened by the light switching off. But in the morning, the light was still on. My heart leapt into my throat. Where was he? Is he not here yet? I put on some jeans, yanked a sweatshirt over my head, and rushed downstairs. I couldn't move fast enough. Where could they be? Does anyone know anything yet? I found Holly in the living room sitting on the couch and asked, "Are they here? Any word?"

"Not yet."

Before I had an emotional breakdown, Holly tried to comfort me. "They are probably on their way. They have to be. If they aren't back by ten, then I'll be worried. But let's not get too worked up yet."

As we waited, people came and went with the same bewildered faces. They didn't have much to say except, "I'm sure they'll be home really soon." Hours passed, and to my horror, ten o'clock arrived. Our questions mounted, and in desperation, we began to organize a plan of action. How do we find them? What measures can we take? Mark and all the camp guides called friends and family for outside support. Scott was the youngest of nine children, so several family members came to form search parties. Other volunteers from Holly and Scott's church took off work to walk up and down rivers and search for the guys or their vehicle. We called the police, who informed the entire area to watch for our husbands and the missing vehicle while the guys' description and a picture of the vehicle saturated the news. Neighbors joined with volunteers from a canoe trip company to search on the Lamoille River.

Within minutes Holly's living room was transformed into search and rescue headquarters. I tried to remember where James had talked about going, and I wracked my brain recalling where we had already searched. As frantic friends and family searched for clues and made plans of action, a numbing fog clouded my mind as I searched for answers. *Is this a dream? Can this really be happening? Are they okay? Will I see him again? That's not an option! I must see him again! I won't let my mind go there. God, where are You? Are You seeing all this? We need Your help—Your eyes. Please, keep them safe. Bring James home to me—soon. You said last night that they were safe in the shadow of Your wings, so please keep them safe.*

We knew that they would have returned or called if they were okay, but Holly and I tried to stay positive anyway. As the time passed, we rationalized that they weren't back because one or both of them was really hurt. This didn't give us peace, and we became even more desperate to find them.

I thought about James's parents—I hadn't called them! I didn't want to either, but I knew I must tell them so they could be praying. This phone call was going to be the hardest I would ever make. I picked up the phone and called his mom, Penny. Her greeting was pleasant; I could hear in her voice that she was delighted to hear from me. How could I tell her that her son was missing? It almost didn't come out of my mouth, but I said, "Penny, you must pray. James and Scott are missing. They went out yesterday afternoon to go canoeing, and they haven't come back!" I helped her make sense of the heavy news she had received, and as we said our tearful goodbyes, I promised to keep her and Jim posted.

By mid-afternoon, groups were searching every trail and every river. I wanted to look with them, but I couldn't risk missing any word on James and Scott's whereabouts. Outside, Scott's brother-in-law Tom gathered others around his truck and spread out a map across the hood. They highlighted the rivers that had been thoroughly checked, and as they planned where to search next, he broke down and cried, letting his tears soak the map. Charles, the owner of the property, couldn't say anything; he just paced and wandered around the camp.

In the midst of the chaos, an unexpected package arrived from Scott, who had ordered it a few days earlier to let Holly know how much he appreciated her work in getting the camp running. It contained romantic candles and a note: "With all my love, thanks for your help." This reminder of his love strengthened our determination.

I had started our laundry the day before, so to keep my mind busy, I continued to wash and fold James's laundry. But the later it became, the more my heart sank. *God, please don't do this to me again. Please! Do You even hear me anymore? I can't live without him. You know how much I love him. I need him. You gave him to me.* But despite my pleading, I only heard silence.

The trooper who was heading up the search from another location stayed in direct contact with us and kept us posted on leads, a few of which had been worth checking. He reassured us that we would be the first to know anything.

A camera crew arrived to do a story for the evening news; we hoped that someone who watched it might know something. In the living room, which had large folding tables covered with maps spread throughout it, the crew prepared to film. I sat speechless and numb to all that was going on around me, and soon the camera crew was ready to film. The lights were on and the camera was rolling when Holly received a call from a local policeman. Scott and James had been found.

She shot a glance at me, letting me know that she was finally getting some information. I sat on the edge of her every word. I had no idea what she was hearing on the other end. But as tears filled her eyes, I knew the news wasn't good. She looked at me and said, "They found them. They were in the river. Both dead." Out of respect, the camera crew stopped filming and once those with us processed the news, the wailing began; I had never before heard such cries. As I sat stunned with disbelief, I shook my head back and forth saying, "No, no!" That's all I could say. Holly bolted out the door, threw herself in the grass, and cried out in anguish.

I went to hide myself, but there was no escape—no use in trying to evade reality.

> Where can I go from Your Spirit? Or where can I flee from Your presence? If I ascend to heaven You are there; If I make my bed in Sheol, behold You are there.
>
> *Psalm 139:7-8 (NAS)*

I sat in a stairwell just off the living room and stared at the walls that surrounded me. *Why did you take him, Lord? Why not me? He was so good. He loved You so much.* I couldn't hide anymore. I knew I had to talk to God—really talk to Him. I walked out the front door and headed for a hill close by. I intended to confront God, but my defenses shut down with every step. I had no power, nothing in my hands, and nothing left in me, but I needed to talk, to question, and to hear His voice. I found a quiet place—a hill away from the noise of weeping—and I looked up to the dark, mysterious sky and fell to my knees. Sitting in the cool grass, without tears or a fist held high, I said, "He was Your gift to me. Why?" On the horizon, storm clouds hung in obedience but not a drop had fallen from their grip. I sensed His presence and His attention, but an eerie silence still filled the air. I sat within the walls of His kingdom, in His throne room, at His mercy. He didn't explain Himself. He didn't have to. He didn't have to do anything, but I heard His voice loud and clear.

> Stand at the crossroads and look. Ask where the good way is, and walk in it, and you will have rest for your souls.
>
> *Jeremiah 6:16 (NAS)*

A crossroad was before me. Which way would I go? I was disappointed in, hurt by, and mad at God for how He had treated me, but in that moment, truth reigned in my heart. I had known the truth but hadn't let it set me free. I had chosen to wear the shackles and believed that by putting them on myself, I would be safe from Him. I had to choose, but there was just two choices: I could choose to run away as hard and as fast as possible or I could run as hard and as fast as I possibly could toward God. I knew the choice was mine. No matter my answer, He was still the same God and would hold the same power, but I heard Him beckoning, "Come."

It happened in a moment, but as I remember, the

time seemed to stand still as I considered my choices. I had denied that outstretched hand so many times in the past eight months because I didn't want to believe that He could be trusted. But now my husband—the person who meant the most to me on this entire earth—was gone, taken in a blink of an eye. What if I chose that road again? If I kept running, turning my back on God—this time for good—where would I end up? I already knew the answer: alone, angry, depressed, bitter, and maybe dead. Did I really think that would solve anything? Would that be the life that I wanted to live—mornings so depressed I wanted death? Would James want me to live in constant defiance or hatred toward God?

Then I pictured myself running back to God, laying my broken life at His feet, prostrate at the King's mercy. I knew I would be received, and right then I was on that "other" road, and it wasn't working out for me. I knew what I had to do. I could only imagine what kind of scolding I would get for how I'd been treating Him, and I'd probably have to work really hard for Him to forgive me, but there was no other choice. He was my only option. I looked up to the sky and I said, "Please, my King, can I come?"

And with those words, the King stepped down from His throne, scooped me up in His arms, and carried me back to His throne. And there in His lap, I wept.

In the year of King Uzziah's death, I saw the Lord sitting on a throne, lofty and exalted, with the train of His robe filling the temple.

Isaiah 6:1 (NAS)

AMONG THE RUINS

Holly

After receiving the news from the sheriff, I looked at Heather, and our worst fears were realized. I didn't know how to respond. How could I tell my sister that her husband was dead? As I gazed into her eyes, she knew. I had to get away from the lights of the film crew. I burst open our front door and threw myself into the wet grass. I cried and wailed. The husband I adored was gone. Emma's daddy would never hold her again or laugh at her face when she sucked on another sour pickle. My rock was missing.

After a time of asking God, "Why?" I felt His sweet Holy Spirit still my questioning and overwhelming sadness. Julie knelt by me, and we prayed and cried together. Suddenly I found myself saying things that I still cannot fully comprehend: "Lord, I love You. Thank you for Your kindness." I heard it coming out of my mouth, but did I really believe it? Thank You for Your kindness? What type of kind God could allow such a thing to happen to two young men? What is kind about tragic death?

❧ *Heather*

When what we value most in this life is suddenly taken from us, in the vulnerability of that moment our eyes are opened to see God a little more clearly. Paul, in 1 Corinthians 13:12, compares what we see of God while on earth as what we might see in a dimly lit mirror—a blurred image—but when we see Him face-to-face, we'll look at Him with 20/20 vision. It was because of death that I could see more clearly. In the year of James's death, I saw the Lord.

Crisis illuminated reality, and that reality brings us face-to-face with God Himself. I took my first step toward Him and into His kingdom. His kingdom had always been there, but I had been unable to live in it because I wanted to live in *my* kingdom, and I couldn't see Him there. For so long I had had a distorted view of God and of the truth, but as I took in His kingdom, scales fell from my eyes, and His nearness collided with my broken will, producing a surrendered heart that fell into whole submission. I was face-to-face with truth.

I am the way and the truth and the life.

John 14:6 (NIV)

A deep slumber had kept me unaware of His presence, but I was finally waking from my grave-like sleep and coming alive—a new creation—never to return to who I once was. I would only be transformed if I learned who He truly was. When you see a glimpse of His face, you see all your imperfections, and you know He sees them too. His eyes passed through my entire being and invaded the most private of places of my heart; they went exactly where I didn't want them to go. *You see right through me. I'm scared of who You are.* I tried to hide, but I wanted to be found. My depravity and humanness screamed for a Savior.

I am ruined!

Isaiah 6:5 (NAS)

Scripture says that no one can see the Lord's face and live. James saw the Lord's face when he left this life to go into the next, and when I caught a glimpse of God that day, I died too. One glimpse of His face, and I had to die—so I could live. Everything that I held dear was gone. I not only lost my father, my husband, and best friend, but I lost my dreams, my plans, my hopes, and my life. The life I had lived just seventy-two hours earlier was nowhere to be found. Running to the One who had taken everything from me seemed crazy, but somehow I knew that only He could bring me through this; only He could take my broken life and in turn resurrect this heart.

> For whoever wishes to save his life will lose it, but whoever loses his life for My sake, he is the one who will save it.
>
> *Luke 9:24 (NAS)*

I was one scarred and scared little girl. My loss left me trembling to the bone. I couldn't stop crying—tears flowed like a river with an ocean as its source. I couldn't stop the pain; it was too deep to medicate and too all-encompassing to determine where it began or where it ended. My life had shattered into a million pieces. *How do I continue to take breath in my body? God, I don't know how to breathe anymore.* I pleaded with the Lord and begged Him to either hold me and never let go or simply allow me to die. I lingered in His embrace, curled up like an infant in my Father's arms. I let Him hold me. Comfort washed over me, but pain's own waves bore down upon me; unable to stand against her, I felt like I was drowning. But His deep called to my deep in the roar of His waterfalls, and they rushed over me, covering my pain. His arms pulled me in tighter to His chest—so tight I could hear His heart. I could tell it wasn't angry; it was breaking with mine. As my heartbeat found His rhythm, my tears whispered thankfulness. *How could You be so good to me right now? I don't deserve any of this. You could have easily left me for dead—that's what I deserve!* As I clung to Him, His tears joined mine. He was hurting with me and for me;

His tears told me that He understood my pain. *Heather, I hurt when you hurt.* When I expected punishment, He surprised me with His love. His heart was grieving on my behalf, and it was His kindness in that moment that led me to repentance (Romans 2:4).

> He stood me up on a wide-open field; I stood there saved—surprised to be loved!
>
> *Psalm 18:19 (MSG)*

Standing in the middle of that field, I experienced God's lovingkindness and power. His response was proof to me that He wasn't going anywhere and that He would stay close. I walked around for a bit and finally found Holly. We needed each other. My pain multiplied again when I saw her, and we held each other. The pain multiplied more when I held little Emma and watched her eyes explore our faces to find answers. "Why are you crying?" She couldn't understand that her daddy and uncle weren't coming home. We could barely comprehend it ourselves.

When the campers from New Jersey heard the news, they gathered together to pray and worship. Holly heard singing from the barn, and she joined them, falling to her knees in worship. As they sang, "I Could Sing of Your Love Forever," she lifted her voice with pure, unreserved worship to the Lord, praising Him despite her pain. For her to respond to God in that moment, in that way, still astounds me. How He must have cherished her in that moment. As her song filled His temple, would He not have hushed the angels' songs? Would He not have silenced their adoration as her voice echoed through heaven's halls? Her song declared her love for God despite her loss and declared her devotion despite the pile of ashes she knelt in. Her offering must have resounded in His ears and brought tears to His eyes as He said, "That's My girl!" The unfailing love He had given to Holly was returned to Him. Instead of turning a fist to the Lord, she lifted her trembling hand and offered her heart. Was she hurting? Yes! Was she disappointed and broken? Yes! But within her arose a need to worship her Lord *in* her pain. That was her dance among her ashes. What a testimony to spur us to worship no matter our circumstances or our loss—even if we don't know why. Can we simply say, "I will sing of Your love forever"? The world certainly won't be able to fathom a response like that; it isn't a natural or a human response. It is a godly response. God stepped in and responded through one who *must* praise Him. One who must praise Him in *all* times—good or bad.

> The Lord gave and the LORD has taken away. Blessed be the name of the LORD.
>
> *Job 1:21 (NAS)*

It was time for me to do the unthinkable: call James's parents. *What will I say? How will I tell them their one and only son is gone. No goodbyes, no last memories, no notice? God, this isn't fair for them!* They were awaiting my call, praying that I had news of their son's safe return, but through my tears, they knew he wasn't coming back. We cried together, and Jim simply said, "I'll be there tomorrow. I'm coming to bring my son home."

Everything was a blur, and everyone on the campground walked around in a daze with no real destination. We struggled to comfort one another because we all carried the same load. Next door in Charles's house, I sat in his library and waited for more news. The troopers whom we had been working with all day had been on their way to deliver the news to us in person when we received the call from another source; they hadn't wanted us to hear it over the phone. While I waited for them to arrive, I made a few emotionless calls to close family and friends and told them what had happened. To get the news out, I had to disengage my mind and my emotions because I had hardly accepted it myself.

When the troopers finally arrived, they gathered Holly and me in the library, took off their hats, and offered their condolences. It was like a scene from a movie where men in uniform come to deliver the very news you dread. And I'm sure they dreaded delivering such news as they stood before two young wives and told them that their husbands weren't coming home. They gave us what little information they had up to that point; they weren't sure what had exactly happened but didn't suspect foul play. James and Scott had been found on a canoe route in Vermont about one hundred feet from where the truck was parked. They both had on their lifejackets, and it looked as though they had been in the process of walking the canoe to the put-in. The oars were still in the vehicle, as were the keys and the bike they had brought to ride back to the truck. None of it made much sense at that hour because we were still in shock, but soon my mind would wrestle with such news. I didn't want to think about the horrific death they had experienced. I wanted to awake from this unimaginable nightmare! We managed to thank the troopers for coming, and they said they'd let us know more as their investigation continued.

I don't remember what happened the rest of the evening; I only remember going to bed. Holly, Emma, and I slept together that night, and it was the longest and worst night of my life. We tossed and turned all night, sobbed ourselves to sleep, and fought off thoughts of what our husbands must have gone through. When I did sleep, my dreams taunted me as I watched the water overtake them with an undertow that held them defenseless. In panic they struggled to survive, and my dreams raged and swallowed me underwater with them. I subconsciously felt the pain they went through—the water, the rocks, their cries—and then I'd awake to hear Holly weeping next to me. The dreams tortured us both, but Emma slept peacefully in between us. We lay there most of the night without saying a word, sometimes just staring at each other. At one point, I think I said, "I can't wake up from this nightmare!"

When the sun began to rise, I was relieved and thankful to have made it through the night; but reality wounded me as I thought about what the day might hold. *Lord, the same torture? The same pain?* Holly surprised me that morning when she woke up and said, "God has placed a song in my heart." She proceeded to sing the old hymn, "The Steadfast Love of the Lord."

Holly

I did not want to get out of bed, but I could see the sun's beams finally shining through my windows. I sat up on my bed, and as my feet hit the floor, I found my spirit singing inside of me. I recalled singing this song a little as a child, but never on a regular basis. I sang this song over and over in my heart all day long as I began dealing with the emotional wreckage left behind in this wake. It brought me such strength.

> *The steadfast love of the Lord never ceases*
> *His mercies never come to an end*
> *They are new every morning, new every morning*
> *Great is Thy faithfulness, O Lord*
> *Great is Thy faithfulness.*[4]

Heather

What a beautiful reminder that God was near and that He was aware of our pain! He hadn't slept peacefully that night and forgotten about us; He had seen our sleepless torture and had been there in every agonizing moment. That morning He wanted us to know that His steadfast love would never cease—it was new that and every morning. He who was faithful would continue to show us His immense faithfulness!

Holly

Even though a song played in my heart and mind, I was still overwhelmed with the arrival of this new day and how it brought more pain. Scott's mom and dad arrived to the campground, and before speaking to anyone, his mom paced outside on the vast lawn behind Charles's house with her face buried in her hands. I gave her a few moments until I couldn't bear it any longer. I went running to her and found myself sobbing in her arms. The strength she exhibited and compassion toward me is something I'll never forget. She said, "The Lord must think a lot of you to allow your daddy and Scott to be taken from you." Her comment surprised me. It wasn't about her pain, but she entered mine. She had just lost her baby—the apple of her eye—yet she desired to encourage me. What love she exhibited in that moment.

Heather

I spent most of the morning staring out the window, letting my mind wander in and out of reality. In one moment, I'd cry so hard that I thought I might throw up, but in the next, I felt as though my tear ducts had dried up, and I believed that I might never shed another tear. But the tears would make their way down my cheeks again. Where they came from, I had no idea.

The campers left to return home to New Jersey, and

as the bus headed out the driveway, I thought, "Well, this wasn't at all what they expected! What a horrific tragedy to witness!" Just like them, none of us had known what was in store for us that week, and I knew we would all continue to process what had transpired.

> Our holy and glorious temple, where our fathers praised You, has been burned with fire, and all that we treasured lies in ruins.
>
> *Isaiah 64:11 (NIV)*

Because we were so devastated, the normalcy of our daily lives was stolen. Sometimes grief would rush over us in the middle of a meal. We knew we had to eat, and everyone would say, "You need to eat *something*." Food was set before me, but even when I gathered enough strength to put my plate together, I would just sit at the table and sob, hovering over my untouched food. I couldn't eat. Others responded the same way: Mark, one of Scott's brothers, made it through his first bite, but in the middle of the next, despair rushed in. Uncontrollable sobbing took over, and there he sat with a mouth full of food, fork in hand, unable to swallow. The normalcy of eating had been stolen, and when one of us would cry publicly, it would knock us all over like dominoes. None of us were able to make it completely through many of those first meals.

Holly

The day following the news of their death, I received a phone call from a dear friend, one of our childhood pastors. He had heard the news, and in his prayer time that morning the Lord brought him to the following Scripture: "O God, listen to my cry! Hear my prayer! From the ends of the earth, I will cry to you for help, for my heart is overwhelmed. Lead me to the rock of safety, for you are my safe refuge, a fortress where my enemies cannot reach me" (Psalm 62:1–3 NLV).

I cannot begin to tell you how I have held onto this verse since that day. Another translation says, "I will cling to the rock that is higher than I." I pictured myself in a great storm being overtaken by waves. The wind picked up, and I held on for dear life. I thought for a time that Scott was my rock—my security—but he couldn't be. That wasn't fair to him, my Creator, or myself. Jesus is that rock. Who can begin to understand our God? I knew of nothing else but I must cling to this rock like never before.

Heather

Later that morning Holly and I decided to go to the site of the accident, so we could try to understand what had happened. We longed for our minds to be at rest, for answers, and were hopeful that the site would help us put some of the pieces together. I don't remember if we drove there by ourselves or if someone else transported us; even now that day remains a blur; but however we got there, we got there together.

At the site we noticed a television crew arriving ahead of us to film the area. A sheriff's deputy showed us where the truck was located and where the bodies were found. Somehow we gathered enough strength to see it all, even the waters that had raged through my nightmares a few hours earlier. The water did not hesitate as it raced downstream; it boasted as if to remind me that it stopped for nothing and no one. Holly and I held hands as we ventured over some rocky terrain that led to a small cliff that overlooked the river. It was dangerous, but we carefully put one foot in front of the other and stepped slowly to the edge. The deputy said, "Imagine these rocks yesterday. It had rained all morning."

Holly and I soaked in our environment, and when I had finally had enough, I said out loud, "James, what were you thinking? Scott, you knew better than this!" Honest anger rushed in as I shook my head in disbelief. I was disappointed that they had put themselves in that position. No, I didn't know all the details, but I imagined them not being as careful as they should have. With no idea of what was about to take place, they probably put their lifejackets on as they talked beside the vehicle. Had they been joking about something that had been said on the radio? Were they reminiscing about James's speeding ticket that morning? Was Scott giving James advice on how to deal with a crazy wife? Did they unload the canoe and begin walking before they noticed the wet and mossy rocks? Why hadn't they been more careful? Did they know that in only a few minutes their earthly lives would leave their bodies? I imagined it to that point but didn't want to go any further.

We asked the deputy what he thought might have happened, and he believed that before they found a spot to put in, one or both of the guys carried the canoe along the rocks that led to the river and slipped. With the oars remaining in the car and how the vehicle had been left, he believed it had been a quick accident. Because it had rained so much on the morning of the accident, the water had been higher and much faster than usual. "One may have fallen in and the other gone in after the other. I'm not quite sure," the deputy said. From Scott's autopsy report, we knew that he had received a relatively deep gash to his head, which may have left him unable to fight the current. But even this was speculative. Law enforcement was still talking to neighbors in the area and asking if anyone had seen anything, but of those with whom they talked, there had been no witnesses.

Confusion washed over me. The water was only five feet deep, so how could two strong men drown in such shallow water? My feeble mind attempted to put the string of puzzle pieces together, but it still didn't make sense.

An employee who worked for a lumber company along the river had noticed their empty canoe early Wednesday but thought little of it until he heard the news of the missing canoeists. He searched near the lumberyard again and found their vehicle. He pointed down the river, "That's where we found them, about a hundred feet from here in that small cove. We found their bodies together." Together. They began their day *together*. They rode off *together* to find this canoe route. They died *together* in this river. Their bodies were found *together* in that small cove. And *together* they entered heaven. A place they had only dreamed about—a place they'd read about but never witnessed with their own eyes—until now. They were *together* now and forever.

At last the peace I desired washed over me and covered me as I sat and imagined that moment. Did they step from this life to the next in a blink of an eye as Scripture describes? Did they see angels in the sky celebrating their homecoming? Were their hearts torn for those they were leaving behind or was it all about going home? Imagining them in heaven planted peace in my heart, which surprisingly produced joy. God used those images—that hope—to put strength in my bones so I could stand up and walk away without diving headlong into the waters myself.

Come, all you who are thirsty, come to the waters.

Isaiah 55:1 (NIV)

That evening my father-in-law, Jim, arrived, and as he and his brother Newt pulled up to the house, they came to *my* rescue while facing *their* own fears. James was not there. How could Jim have known that when he waved goodbye to his son earlier that summer, he was saying goodbye here on earth? We didn't say much; we simply sat together and wished things were different. *How has it come to this?* Even though seeing Jim's face gave me much comfort, his eyes were full of pain, and my heart felt it. My heart reminisced as I fought back images of them together, laughing and joking. Their days had been stolen. Never on this earth would they again greet each other with their usual giant hug.

Those thoughts were too much for me, and I knew that my mind needed rest. I squeezed my eyes shut and begged my mind to turn from those agonizing thoughts; I petitioned God to sweep over me.

There was much to do the next day, so we decided to go to bed and try to get some sleep. But I dreaded the night; it had tortured me like never before, and the thought of going back to that place sent shivers up my spine; but God gently reminded me of Holly's song. It *had* surprisingly given me physical evidence that God was with us, keeping us going. She and I were exhausted mentally, physically, and emotionally, and we were ready for sleep to overtake us. Though we didn't sleep peacefully, we did manage to get through another night of fighting off our wicked enemy—our own destructive minds. With every nightmare, we awoke to the harsh reality that our husbands were not there to take us into their arms, to hold us, and to tell us everything was going to be all right. I pleaded with God to let me awake and see James's eyes and his smile; but when I came to, all I saw was the cold room.

As we planned our day the next morning, we had hopes, as torturing as it sounds, of seeing James's body, but the coroners advised us to wait until we were back in Missouri. Because of the nature of his death, the extensive autopsy had lasted a bit longer than usual, and because we were traveling out of state for the funeral, the body had not been prepared for viewing. Jim was the only one who went ahead and saw James's body; after discussing it, Jim and Newt suggested I had been through enough and advised me to wait.

That afternoon we sat down with Brent Hallenbeck, a writer for *The Burlington Free Press*. Because so much had been broadcasted about the guys, others were curious about what had transpired, how we were doing, and what we expected might happen to the Pathway Ministries Camp. I was hesitant to talk because I didn't think I would physically be able to get through it, but Holly and I decided that we couldn't pass up the opportunity to share God with the people of that area. That's why camp was there; it existed to be a light. Even though everything in us wanted to retreat, God gave us the strength to speak in detail concerning the painful events that had just transpired. God blessed us with a writer who really listened to what we were saying and who was patient and kind.

Holly, Jim, and I sat at the kitchen table and told our story. We were not speaking out of our own strength, and in our complete and absolute weakness, God shined. By His grace we made it through the entire interview. Sometimes we had to stop and just cry, but we managed to hold on to one another and press through some of the details. I loved talking about the men they were. I believed the world could have benefited from knowing them, so I cherished sharing their memory.

As the interview ended, we prayed that God would receive glory and that others might catch a glimpse of the lives our young husbands had lived. We were a bit nervous to see how we would be portrayed, but the story on the front page of Sunday's paper overwhelmed us with its accuracy and its direct emphasis on our faith. Even the headline screamed that we were Christians: "Loss of two canoeists tests families' faith." The article spoke of their fire for God, the history of the camp, the accident, and how we were responding.

Holly shared how she had run out of the house, cried for a while, and later "thanked God for his kindness." How many heads shook in disbelief when they read that statement? How many people wondered, "How could she thank God? He just left her a widow." That article gave *me* hope. Hope that good could come from such tragedy. Hope that others could know Scott and James's God. Hope that they could know *my* God and experience His love, His power, His sovereignty, and His pursuit. Did strangers grasp that they could absolutely have a relationship with One who would never leave or forsake them—One who promised to hold them close even when their world fell around them? I clung to the very One who could have stopped the tragedy. It might not have made sense, but I knew I'd die without Him. I pressed into Him further with more force. I had to be closer. I had to hide myself in this God. I had to trust Him with the days ahead.

His huge outstretched arms protect you- under them you are safe; his arms fend off all harm.

Psalm 91:4 (MSG)

Jim, Newt, and I prepared to return to Missouri, but it was hard to fathom leaving Vermont without James beside me. I hadn't imagined leaving like this, but I was ready to go home. As the three of us got on our plane and headed for Missouri, we had no idea what was in store for us. With many hang-ups and plane malfunctions, the day was excruciatingly long. I thought I'd never see the outside of an airport again.

When we first left Vermont, I sat by myself on the plane and pulled out a book I had brought with me. When my dad passed away, I had been reading *The Eye of the Storm* by Max Lucado, but I had picked it up only a handful of times since then. The last time I read it, I just got angry at God if I felt a prick from the words on the page; this time I let the tears fall and let the words take root in my heart. I forgot about everyone else on the plane, and I wept before the Lord. God was using the words on the page to speak right into my situation, and I knew that He wanted me to speak at James's funeral. I pulled out a piece of paper and began writing what I was going to say. The words came easily, and I knew that God was prompting me so I could not only love on James publicly but so God could do something bigger. I didn't question it; I just said, "I'll do it." A song that I had heard prior to James's death came to my mind and stirred me in places where only God could reach. I knew that I must sing "Job" by Cindy Morgan as worship to God at the funeral. I wasn't sure if I'd be able to, but I promised to walk forward in faith and to let God carry the yoke upon my neck.

Layovers! They left me with nothing to do and

nothing to think about except my pain; the waiting intensified my ache. With too much time on my hands, my mind wandered and tortured me as I sat with nothing to hold my attention. My mind journeyed and made me believe things were as they had once been. Sometimes I could almost picture James walking toward me; I would see someone with a similar build and imagine it was James. I felt like I was going crazy because it felt so real, as if I was literally seeing *him*. But as the dreaming became reality, pain broke my heart all over again. *God, help me! I miss him!*

At one point we had a layover that was supposed to last one hour but turned into four. When the airline finally let us board, they made us get off because of a plane malfunction. After telling us we'd be able to board in thirty minutes, we sat there for another two hours. Most people were a little nervous, wondering if we would make it home safely, but at that point, I couldn't have cared less! I was in such anguish that I wasn't concerned if I survived or not. When we finally arrived in Missouri, the airline had lost our luggage, which about sent us all over the edge. After expressing our frustration, we left the airport with an hour and a half of driving to endure. We arrived well after 2:00 a.m.—drained and exhausted, empty shells of who we once were.

As we neared the house, fear gripped my heart. I had agonized over coming to *his* house off and on during our trip. His house full of all those memories! How in the world could I walk in without him by my side? Penny quickly met us, and we hugged for a long time.

Jim quickly pulled us apart and suggested that we all try to get some sleep; we were all exhausted. I climbed in bed with Stacy, James's youngest sister.

> I am weary with crying; my throat is parched; My eyes fail while I wait for my God.
>
> *Psalm 69:3 (NAS)*

The next few days were a blur. I can't tell you in what sequence everything happened; I just know it happened. In the midst of planning for the funeral, we did a lot of crying and a lot of loving on one another, and we even tried our best to laugh a little—thinking about James's life didn't make that too hard. In his life he had lived for laughs, leaving us with many memories of silliness and excitement; and with these memories, our tears would mingle with our laughter. We tried our best to comfort one another without lingering too long on the whys. It felt good to be with family, even though there was a constant reminder that something—someone—was missing. This gaping hole couldn't be filled with the gifts we received—and others knew that—but they still offered what they could with plants, flowers, food, and hugs. Solemn faces of grieving friends were in and out; some brought their condolences with tears streaming down their cheeks, while others struggled to make eye contact. No visitor stayed long, just long enough to shake their heads in disbelief.

At some point I found myself walking through a room filled with caskets again, choosing a place to lay his lifeless body. I felt like I had been there just yesterday helping choose my father's casket. I felt sick, weak, and angry; but by God's gentle grace, I continued on. When I felt like my legs were giving out from under me, He'd hold me up. When I'd get to my breaking point, saying, "I can't do this!" He'd say, "It's okay. I'm here. Let Me help you." Before I knew it, love would rush in and take over.

A friend from college came to be with me. I had called her from Vermont, and she told me later that it was a phone call that made her head spin for a long time. We were friends in college but had been closer to others, yet when I called and told her about the accident, I asked her what she was doing the following week; she had already planned to be on vacation. I asked her if she would come and be with me during the funeral and the days leading up to it. My mom and most of my family were traveling, trying to make it to both funerals, and I needed someone who could be with me.

Carrie and I had always had a special relationship filled with laughter and fun, and something in me knew that I needed to be around that kind of friend: someone I could cry with, but more importantly, someone who would offer some joy in the midst of my tears. Looking back, I really don't know why I asked this of her; it seems so unreasonable now—quite a heavy request— but I believe God brought her to all of us for a reason! She was such a blessing to me and Stacy. She let us rant and rave and in the next moment be quiet and just sit next to her as she played with our hair. We were all so wounded that we couldn't offer to one another what we all needed ourselves. God brought Carrie to me so

I could share things that I didn't feel comfortable saying to the Brills for fear that I would bring them more pain. This way I could be mad and selfish, and Carrie just listened and gently pointed me toward the Lord. Carrie had also had a special relationship with James—a rivalry if you will—full of great memories of friendly banter and priceless renditions of her favorite southern gospel singers. She brought a piece of his comedy back into my life.

A load was lifted when she came to be with me, but the ongoing heaviness weighed on my heart, and in light of the upcoming services, I needed to busy myself with the things that would pay tribute to my husband—and bring honor to the God he loved. I compiled some family photos and some of my favorite pictures of us, and we made a collage of pictures to be displayed at the visitation and funeral. We also displayed an album of photographs from places James had explored and the beauty of God's creation that he had witnessed.

> Surely the arm of the LORD is not too short to save,
> nor his ear too dull to hear.
>
> *Isaiah 59:1 (NIV)*

I had to see James one last time to say my goodbyes. We weren't able to have an open casket during his services because of the manner in which he died, but I hadn't seen his face in so long. I didn't know whether I was excited to see him again or whether fear would overpower my heart. I knew it wasn't him anymore; the body I saw was simply the tent in which he lived among us. But when I looked upon his lifeless body, there was finality; my heart begged James to open his eyes and for this all to be some crazy nightmare. As everyone left me to be alone with him, I couldn't look at him anymore. The body before me wasn't him, and I didn't want that image engrained in my mind. I stood beside him one last time, just he and I, and I closed my eyes and prayed. I thanked God for taking him home. Without thinking about it, I lifted my hand in worship, praising God, confessing that I didn't understand but had to trust Him from that moment on. In every moment, I had to surrender again and again and again. If I didn't, the pressure to fall, to get angry, to shake my fist, would become too strong. Standing at his casket with my left hand raised, I praised my God. I was learning to dance.

> Then Job arose and tore his robe and shaved his head, and he fell to the ground and worshiped.
>
> *Job 1:20 (NAS)*

By God's strength and power, I made it through the services. The visitation was difficult. There were many people that I didn't know, so making conversation was draining. Others would share a hug and tell me how they knew "Jamie" (as the whole town would say), and it was sweet to hear their stories. At the oddest times I would lose it and weep right there in front of strangers; other times there would be no tears, and I'd feel guilty because I wasn't crying. My heart ached each time I caught a glimpse of one of his friends, and my pain would double as I realized what they had lost as well. I did as well as I could. I reminded myself that this is not a comfortable place for anyone.

This reminder was helpful especially when people said or did things that were plain stupid. My sister experienced some of this as well, and we joked later that we were going to write a book of things you don't say at a visitation. This would be a chapter: "A Widow at Twenty-three? How Horrible!" One older woman said this to me over and over and over, and part of me thought she kept saying it because I didn't cry the first five times she said it. She proceeded to remind me of my state in life until I did cave. I'm sure she meant well.

I took a deep breath and prepared myself for the funeral service. That morning, God took such sweet care of me. I felt Him all over me, and I knew it was Him when I woke up with a smile on my face. He used so many of my friends to love on me: some did my hair, while others held my hand. My sister Heidi did my makeup, which we had to apply at least three different times. I wanted to look pretty for my husband one last time.

God showed up that day. The church was packed with those who came from all over to celebrate the life of James Michael Brill. The processional was almost too much for me to bear. My poor mom and grandparents had flown to New York for Scott's funeral and had made it back just in time to walk in with us at James's service. I remember looking at my mom and saying, "I don't think I can do this!" She said, "We'll go together." It seemed like I was walking the green mile. The distance was too great, and everyone knew what awaited me at the end: I was burying my love. And part of me would go in the ground that day as well.

We worshiped. We celebrated. We grieved. We loved. Even though it felt surreal and wrong, the service proceeded, and God overpowered me. It was perfect. Have you experienced perfection? A moment when God shines through you, and it's just perfect?

When my time came to speak, my legs moved before I was ready, but I stood by His Spirit. God had called me to praise Him in front of the congregation, and I spoke in submission and adoration. He gave me the chance to love James out loud, but more importantly, He gave me the chance to love God out loud. It was healing. It was my dance for Him. I knew I couldn't do it, but I had to. I witnessed His strength, for it wasn't in me to do what I did that day, so I boasted on a display of God's power, strength, and love. He loved those in the room—those I called stranger, He called sought after. He was pursuing hearts, healing hurts, and challenging faiths. He was calling us all to Himself that day. I sang the words of Job:[5]

Where were You
When my night fell
Pieces shattered everywhere
If I'd have loved You with my whole heart
Time will tell
Time will tell
Were the stars moving across the ocean
Did the world turn away for just a glance
And leave me here in these ashes
I will weep, and I will dance
All I have is Yours
All these ashes and these sores
All that I am living for

I will follow You to shore
Well I hear Your voice and it sounds angry
I have questioned You time and again
So I'll be here in the silence
'Till I can walk, I will stand
All I have is Yours
All these ashes and these sores
All that I'm living for
I will follow You
I will follow You
I will follow You to shore

James had impacted so many lives, and the sea of faces in front of me was a testimony to his life. We remembered him; then we buried him. Our car led the caravan to the graveyard, and I was the first ushered in to sit in those dreaded comfortable seats at the burial site. I loathed the moments of being first. I felt alone. Singled out. Forgotten. But then God would rescue me with some of my favorite words in Scripture, reminding me that He was with me, walking with me, sitting with me, and holding my hand. James would no longer comfort me—I had to trust God with my hand, with my steps, and with my heart. I couldn't rely on James's smile to lighten my load; I would have to rely on the Father's smile. I had to rely on His love to calm my mind and ease my anxious heart.

> Now you've got my feet on the life path, all radiant from the shining of your face.
>> Ever since You took my hand, I'm on the right way.

> *Psalm 16:11 (MSG)*

As I buried my husband, Holly buried hers.

Holly

Scott's sister Julie and I headed from Vermont to New York, and we drove most of the way in silence. Julie turned on the radio to get our minds off the situation at hand, even if it was for a moment, but we began to hear a comedian who was one of Scott's favorites. I began to laugh but moments later I couldn't listen anymore. It seemed that everything that once brought joy now brought pain. But I could still hear God's still, small voice saying, "Everything is going to be okay. Rest in me."

> Rest in the Lord and wait patiently for Him.
>
> *Psalm 37:7 (NAS)*

The day before we buried him, Scott's two best friends, Mark and Andy, wanted to see his body. Scott's family had made the decision to not have a viewing, so I took them to the funeral home. They gave me a chance to see him first, and honestly, I stood there looking at him like he was a stranger. Nothing seemed familiar. Mark and Andy came closer and began to weep. Seeing him there really solidified the great loss of their friend. Questions raced through my mind: *Scott, I know you're not there, but can you see me? How will I ever make it without you? Do you miss me at all?*

The family, close friends, and my pastor I had grown up with all made our way to the burial site, and we quietly gathered around the casket. I wish I could remember more of what happened as we stood there. I don't know if anyone sang, read Scripture, or shared thoughts, but what I do remember completely changed my life forever. I walked up to Scott's casket alone, and I knelt in silence for a moment and prayed silently. As I finished, deep inside my heart I heard God's voice. *Holly, My child, this is just the beginning of your ministry.* I heard it so clearly that I thought everyone gathered around me heard it too. I got up from my knees, ran over to my childhood pastor, and said to him, "Lowell, you will never guess what I just heard the Lord speak to me! He said this was just the beginning of my ministry." My pastor smiled wide, and with reassurance in his eyes, said, "I heard it too."

After the burial we continued to the memorial service at Yates Baptist Church. The place was packed—beyond standing room only. People from everywhere had gathered to pay their respects to the family and to Scott's memory. The service began, and I felt compelled to share. Jennifer Nesbitt, Scott's niece, sang a beautiful song, and many wiped tears from their eyes. She ministered to so many of us. I shared some thoughts and recounted how the Lord had been encouraging me with song and Scripture since Scott's untimely death. I did not shed one tear that day. I couldn't. I overheard people saying that I was in denial and that people needed to keep their eye on me, but I knew what was happening. I was well aware of my and my daughter's loss, but there was an inner peace that permeated me. I felt as though the Lord had put up a strong shelter around every side of me to carry me through those painful moments.

> Whom have I in heaven but You? I desire You more
> than anything on earth. My health may fail, and my
> spirit may grow weak, but God remains the strength
> of my heart; He is mine forever.
>
> *Psalm 73:25–26 (NLT)*

Several people gave their lives to the Lord that day during the service, and this brought such joy and strength to me. I knew that God could "cause all things to work together for good" (Romans 8:28).

We had a second memorial service in Vermont, which was also an encouragement to me, as countless testimonies of how Scott had helped them came forward from friends and strangers—stories he had never told me. I realized there were amazing things about my husband that I did not know, but I felt completely wrapped in warmth and love from our church home there in Barre, Vermont. I am so thankful for the time we shared together.

LIFE AFTER DEATH

Heather

After the funeral, I wish I could say that I was relieved; but grief continued to haunt me, and sorrow became my companion. The service was over, and I was left with the stinging reminder that James was gone and was never coming back. I went home, but in reality, I had no home. My home had been with James, and all our belongings were tucked away in a storage unit ready for our move to Texas.

Holly

They say home is where the heart is, but I didn't know where to find my heart. Parts of me were left in Vermont. Other pieces were in New York. I felt like I was letting everyone down for not staying and seeing Pathway Ministries back to its feet again. The emptiness felt so great, but I was thankful for Emma, who played such an important role in my recovery. She could always make me smile when joy seemed unfathomable. Caring for her did not allow me to mope all day like I really wanted to; she still needed to be fed, and her diapers still needed to be changed. She needed constant love from a mom who needed to make her feel like she was the center of the world.

Heather

I packed my suitcases and headed back to Jefferson City to live with my mom and siblings. There wasn't room for me at first, so I slept with my mom and filled my father's side of the bed. He was supposed to be there with her, but it became my place—yet another severe reminder that things were different and imperfect.

When you are in the middle of a dream, it's funny how your brain has to come up with some reason why someone you love is gone, where they might have been, what were the reasons that deterred them, reasons why they never could make contact. My dreams were often nightmares. Some were a response to crying myself to sleep, and some were a response to my anxiety over the question, "What now?"

I had good dreams too. These dreams brought me back to Vermont, where James and Scott would drive down the gravel road, while I would run outside to see if it was really them. James, looking more like a mountain man—with a full beard and clothes that didn't seem to have been washed in weeks—than the man I married, would get out of the vehicle and grab me and twirl me around, telling me about their long journey home. I would tell him all that we had gone through, that we believed they were dead, and how others came to know the Lord because of their deaths, and I would apologize for being mad about the speeding ticket. But when I awoke to learn my dream was not reality, my nightmare really began—the daylight ushered in the beginning of my daily *lifemare*. I would wake to find my mom next to me sleeping, and I would role over angry, frantically trying to get back into my dream, where I could see him again. But I was never able to close my eyes tight enough to escape back to my dreams.

I had other dreams where James would come back, and we'd have conversations about heaven. I'd ask him what he did all day, what he had seen, and if the streets were as beautiful as I pictured them to be. He wouldn't say much, but his smile and his eyes were radiant and spoke volumes to my heart's questions. Sometimes he'd just smile and say, "You won't believe it even if I told you." Those dreams brought me peace.

Some dreams, however, were worse than the nightmares daylight brought; I dreamt again of watching their deaths. Satan used those dreams to torment me, for I would watch as they struggled, and there was nothing I could do to save them.

> Save me, O God, For the waters have threatened my life. I have sunk in deep mire, and there is no foothold; I have come into deep waters, and a flood overflows me.
>
> *Psalm 69:1–2 (NASB)*

> When you pass through the waters, I will be with you; and when you pass through the rivers, they will not sweep over you. When you walk through the fire, you will not be burned; the flames will not set you ablaze.
>
> *Isaiah 43:2 (NIV)*

These verses gave me no comfort. God promised to hear their cries and *not* let the waters sweep over them, but I was reminded that the waters *had* swept over them. Those verses spoke of a God who will rescue those who are scared for their lives; when the waters rage, He will be the One to call upon. He told me to not fear because He was aware and He was with me; but the evil one did what he could to destroy my faith with these verses. He would say, "God didn't care when James called out for help. If God didn't save him when the waters were overtaking him, he won't save you now. God was able, but He did nothing. His promises are obviously not true! He didn't care." Anger, resentment, and doubts about who God claimed to be provoked me to reject

Him once and for all. It was a battle. The verse in Isaiah taunted me in book after book; it was supposed to bring the grieving comfort and peace, yet the feeling that welled up in my heart was quite the opposite.

Certain verses may stir up some pain in you as well. Maybe you've lost a child. Do you cringe when you hear verses on God's protection? Maybe you're living a life of disappointment, and when you come across verses like, "'For I know the plans I have for you,' declares the Lord, 'Plans to prosper you, and not to harm you, plans to give you a hope and a future'" (Jeremiah 29:11), you feel as though He's failed to remember you or His promises.

I thought it was a coincidence that I kept running into these verses. They seemed to stick out like a sore thumb, and I would push them away because I was trying really hard to be at peace with God and His decisions. But the next day, I'd see them again and read them over and over. There was no use trying to deny what He was saying there, for there it was in black and white. Job had asked the same question that stirred in me: Why didn't God stop this? I had to know. Looking back now, I see that God was not bringing me to these verses over and over to hurt me but to take me down the road to healing.

Our church's youth minister asked Holly and I to come in and talk to him, and I cried in Mike's office when he told us that the Lord had given him verses for us—as he read them aloud, they were the same verses I struggled with. And I cried a lot. *God, what are you doing to me? Are you jabbing the knife in a bit farther and twisting it so I remember that it's there?* I knew God was trying to show me something; He wanted to reveal His heart and show me the answer to my question. Without the truth, I wouldn't really be able to trust Him, and I would be captive to an unhealthy fear that would cause me to submit to Him without love. He wanted me to see the truth and love in His words.

First of all, the truth: *Heather, I heard them.* He *was* aware. He hadn't dozed off only to find them standing at His gates, ready to come in when He awoke. He hadn't been so engulfed with the angels' songs that He had forgotten to watch out for them. He hadn't been hanging out with Abraham, Isaac, and Jacob and not noticed the time. He had heard their cries for help, for nothing happened that day without his knowledge or permission. God is the ultimate multi-tasker. Here's the biggest understatement I could make right now: He can do more than one thing at a time. Scriptures speak of His awareness—that He even knows when a sparrow's life has ended and the number of hairs on my head.

God spoke to my heart again: "The moment James and Scott cried out for help, I came to their rescue!"

"But how could that be?" I snapped back. "If that were true, I wouldn't be sitting here having this conversation with You!" I was overcome by emotion.

But peace swept over me immediately; when my own water's undertow tried to pull me under, peace enclosed me, and He rescued me from the waters that meant to take my life. In that moment, I knew what He meant: Whether physical water or the world's lies pulled me under, He wanted me to call out to Him.

He *would* hear. He *would* rescue. He saved me from drowning in the fateful waters of doubt, despair, hopelessness, and betrayal that day; and even though I didn't understand it at that time, I knew that His thoughts toward saving me were a far greater mystery than my little mind could comprehend. Losing our life might be the very saving that He intends to bless us with.

James and Scott had indeed been rescued. I don't understand it all, and I can't claim to, but I do know that Jesus conquered death long ago. Their deaths were not their end. Their lives here on earth, in God's opinion, were completed, and the day they went under water to never again breathe in earth's gift of oxygen, they were escorted into life as it was intended. They drank in the view, filled their chests with the scents of heaven, and were covered in ultimate peace—the peace that I felt for a mere fraction of a moment here on earth would undeniably carry me through many moments to come.

A few days after the accident, a gentleman who was working on the campgrounds shared with us that he had been the one to identify the bodies at the river. It was one of the hardest things that he had been asked to do, he said, but their faces surprised him. "They both had a certain expression that was very peaceful. It almost looked as if they were slightly smiling." God had rescued them. God hadn't let the waters sweep over them that day. He *had* kept His promises.

In the Bible, the apostle Stephen encountered fulfillment of this promise too. At the end of his life—in the midst of men ready to stone him—Scripture says he looked up to heaven and saw Jesus standing at the right hand of the Father. Stephen wasn't alone. He wasn't being overtaken; he was being rescued. God was not only aware; He was there. And where was Jesus? Not on the edge of His seat; He was standing. Standing for his friend and welcoming Stephen into His glory. Stephen wasn't looking to save his life on earth; he knew that to be rescued meant far more than dodging stones. As rocks were hurled at his head and chest and forced him to his knees, Stephen prayed for the very ones who were casting those rocks, and Scripture says, "He fell asleep" (Acts 7:60).

A good friend of mine described to me the moment her father went to be with the Lord. He was dying of cancer, and the family was gathered around the bed. They'd been there for days—waiting, praying, and trying hard to hold themselves together. She said the moment was unforgettable. Peacefully, her father opened his eyes, and without many words, said goodbye. He looked to his wife, his three daughters, his son, his son- and daughters-in-law, and each of his grandchildren. Blowing a kiss to each one, he closed his eyes and said one word: Jesus!

God was a lot of things that I needed Him to be, and I began to recognize that He truly was love. I could trust His heart, and I didn't have to ask why. Did I have other questions rising up within me? Sure. The answers were not for my understanding, but I could have confidence that this love was real and that it would carry me through the questions. I knew that I wouldn't make it in the days ahead without Him; I had to cling to Him with all I had if I wanted to survive. God knew that, which is why He knew that I needed to come face-to-face with whom it was that I was clinging so I could have peace that He was good. I was scared to death to be without Him. My mind would wander back to how I had previously responded to Him, and I was mortified, embarrassed, and sad. Here He was giving me peace, comfort, even laughter with my family, and I knew that couldn't be on my own. It was His Spirit filling me up, coming to my aid when all I could do was cry.

> When my heart was grieved and my spirit embittered, I was senseless and ignorant; I was a brute beast before You.
>
> *Psalm 73:21–22 (NIV)*

I had been an ignorant, horrible, prideful mess. I called into question all I believed and thought I knew about God, but with my false god stripped away, God revealed His true character to me. I saw Him, and He was good—perfect. He hurt when I hurt, yet He was comfortable to let me suffer, but He was never comfortable leaving me to my own demise. He pursued me so I could find real life. He was no longer Santa Claus; the red jacket and goofy chuckle had all been fragments of my imagination, and He wasn't checking to see if I was naughty or nice. He was sovereign. Sovereign is defined as a ruler or permanent head of a state, especially a king or queen. I had never met a king, and I don't know if I ever will on this side of heaven.

An introduction to God meant an introduction to not any king but *the* King, and I had been rude and ridiculous in His presence. I deserved to be thrown out of His courts, banished from His presence, and killed for the accusations I had brought against Him. I was humbly aware of this, but He responded with love not wrath, and He wanted to introduce me to the real King of kings, the Sovereign Lord, the One, the only Jesus. Did I deserve it? Do any of us? No, but He knew I needed to begin knowing Him, and He introduced Himself to me through love.

SORROW MIXED WITH LAUGHTER

A joyful heart is good medicine.

Proverbs 17:22 (NASB)

Laughter can conceal a heavy heart, but when the laughter ends, the grief remains.

Proverbs 14:13 (NLV)

He will once again fill your mouth with laughter and your lips with shouts of joy.

Job 8:21 (NLV)

Going home to my mom's was the right thing to do, but the plan, as it had been in years past, was not simply to come home for the weekend—I was coming home for good. When my family is together, we're always laughing, being silly, and loving on one another, and my sisters are like a spring rain; they make me grow and make me feel loved. They are companions made for me.

Heidi and her husband, Jacob, lived in Colorado, but they hadn't lived there long; they had moved there a couple weeks after our dad passed away. After the funerals, they came back home with us and stayed a few days, but we all knew they'd be leaving soon. Heidi was pregnant and due in little over a month, and she really wasn't supposed to be traveling. As the day approached for their journey back home, we all cried. I had a hard time dealing with another goodbye. Heidi and Jacob came into my room and sat with me on the bed, and we all three wept, knowing there was nothing we could do about it. It was hard on all of us. Heidi hurt for us, and the distance tore her heart out as much as it did mine. Jacob hurt as well. He was the man in the family now. All the others had been taken, and I think his God-given instincts rose up in him; he wanted to protect us, but how could he so far away? We made our tearful goodbyes, and Jacob promised that he would do what he could to bring his family back as soon as he could.

Listen to how good our God is! When they returned home, there was a message on their answering machine from Jacob's company—they wanted to transfer him to the store in Columbia, Missouri, in a few weeks and wanted to know if he was interested. They could be thirty minutes away! He didn't have to make a single call to beg them to consider a transfer; it had all been in the hands of someone bigger, someone who knew what we needed before we asked. Jacob couldn't explain it. He couldn't fathom how it happened or why the company called him out of the blue, but we all knew God knew what we needed, and we praised Him! It was a physical reminder that God was alive and active! Jacob and Heidi were back to Missouri within two weeks. Everything happened so quickly that they were in Jefferson City before they had time to find a place to call home, so they too moved in with the family. Holly and Emma had spent some time with Scott's family in New York before heading home, but within a matter of weeks, there we all were—back home. All nine of us were crammed in that house with one more on the way!

Every couch was taken. Hunter slept in a sleeping bag, while Holly and Emma shared his twin bed. There were three widows under one roof! Sometimes we would look around and shake our heads and cry for one another. Other times we'd laugh because it felt so surreal! Laughter was truly good medicine. Not everyone could laugh with us; they probably didn't think things we laughed about were funny, and I can totally understand that, but we had to laugh at our situation. We laughed at our tears, our struggles, and our houseful. We entertained ideas of having our answering machine answer: Sorry we missed your call. If you would like to leave a message for Widow #1, press 1; for Widow #2, press 2; or for Widow #3, press 3. We could barely believe what we had experienced in the last twelve months, and I think the Lord knew that we needed one another to get through this. Being with family brought laughter, which brought healing for a moment, and many times we'd laugh even while tears streamed down our cheeks, but it was therapeutic.

A NEW SONG

The Lord gave us another gift: music. We didn't have much to take our minds off our situation, so I started looking for distractions. My mom listened to Christian radio before she went to bed and left it on during the night, and the station had been announcing a Labor Day weekend Christian music contest for the listening area. I heard the announcement so often and thought why not? I probably should have asked them first, but I needed a project, so before my sisters had officially moved in, I entered us. For a Christmas present to our family and as a tribute to our father, we had recorded a few songs in our friend's basement a few months prior, so I simply sent in the recording. I didn't know that we'd actually qualify.

When the station asked me what our group was called, I had no idea what to say. I think I said The Walls, which sounded like we were a southern gospel group, but I hadn't been prepared for that question. They ended up referring to us as The Wall Sisters, which made us sound even more southern-gospelish! After gently telling my sisters what I had gotten us into, we decided to go through with it, for we agreed that it might give us something to focus on other than our pain. We had always enjoyed using music to worship the Lord, but singing together had not been a luxury while we lived so far apart. We began practicing, and there was something healing as we sang those songs to the Lord through our grief.

On the day of the concert, I honestly didn't know if I would be able to put the microphone to my mouth; none of us could believe we were actually going through with it. Heidi was nine months pregnant, and it was only five weeks after the accident! Even now, I don't know what I was thinking! I about hyperventilated before we sang; I missed James so much and couldn't understand why I had pushed myself—all of us—into the competition. Heidi found me and gave me a pep talk. We prayed together and decided we'd just close our eyes and sing to the Lord. We barely made it through, but we did well enough to be in the top three. We performed a second song, and we got second place, probably receiving a few pity votes. For each one of us, though, it actually felt really good to feel God's pleasure over us as we sang, and I knew that He had brought us there—as crazy as the timing sounded.

A few months later, during one particular Sunday night worship service, I surrendered my heart once again to the Lord, leaving it completely bare for the Lord to do with it as He pleased. I felt that He and I were the only ones in the room, and there was nowhere else I would have rather been than standing in that moment in His sweet presence. I felt His rays of mercy and love wash over me as I continued to lay my burdens at His feet in worship. Almost like a little girl with a new dress on, my heart was dancing in Him. My spirit was spinning and soaring in His presence. I had a new sense that this exchange of love was far more intimate than any worship experience I had felt before.

I came home that night and shared with my mom how I was feeling during worship. "Mom, I can't put my finger on it, but there's something very different when I'm worshiping." We both marveled at His goodness, and I went to bed that night with satisfaction and contentment. I felt that He was mine and that I was His. For the first time in months, I went to bed with a smile on my face. He was teaching me that He was sovereign in my sorrow.

The very next day I received a letter from Scott's sister-in-law JoAnn. On the letter was a separate attached note, which read, "Holly, I've been holding onto this for a while and felt like now was the right time I was to send it." I proceeded in opening the second letter. "Holly, the Lord wanted me to tell you that your worship to Him right now is rich and precious."

Could it be? My heart leapt. Was it possible that I had something to offer the Lord that was rich and precious to Him? The God of the universe who created all things said I was offering something to Him that was of worth? I ran to my mom with the letter in hand and screamed, "This is it! This is it! This is what

I had trouble expressing about the connection I'm feeling when I'm worshipping Him right now."

Heather

The Lord began awakening something special within me as well. Before he died, James and I had started writing songs together. I had been writing lyrics, and they were coming again. At some level, I desperately wanted to process what was going on in my heart, and I quickly realized that the Lord was prompting this divulgence of my thoughts and my pain, so I thought I might write them on paper to bring me healing and to help me process.

WITH EYES CLOSED

I'm in my car
Streetlights look more blurred than yesterday
The rain falls hard
Should I pull off the road and plan a short stay?
Your side's empty
Is that how it's supposed to be?
Asking, "Why?" is so tempting
With my face in hands, I close my eyes to see
With my eyes closed, I feel you
With my eyes closed, I see you
With eyes closed, everything becomes nothing
And nothing becomes everything
I'm in my mind
Thoughts inside seem more blurred than yesterday
The tears fall hard

Should I turn them off or lift my voice to pray?
His side's still empty
Is this really how it's supposed to be?
Asking why, how tempting!
With my face in hands, I close my eyes to see
With my eyes closed, will I still see you?
With my eyes closed, will I still feel you?
With my eyes closed, everything becomes nothing
And nothing becomes everything
With my eyes closed, Lord I see You
With my eyes closed, Lord, I feel You
With my eyes closed

A friend gave me a journal, and I started journaling in it; this surprising gift continued my journey towards healing that I hadn't expected.

December 27, 2000

Romans 10:11 says, "Whoever believes in Him will not be disappointed." I feel that speaks for my life because I've always believed this to be true, yet I'm struggling with believing it now. I know in my head that it is true, but my heart is playing catch-up.

In a letter to James I wrote:

I'm still trusting that this was for the best even though it sure stinks beyond belief now. You were so great at everything you did. I sure wish I had died and not you. You would have done so much better as a role model for other believers had things been different. If you can, encourage the Lord to come quickly; I feel useless down here.

January 22, 2001

I would love to disintegrate into this air.
Would anyone care?
Or dare, tell me there's more here for me?
It just couldn't be.
I just couldn't see that side of things from here.
I must keep on living
And thank God for giving
One more day.
A day to throw up my hands -
Stop shouting demands
Of which I think I deserve!
I must not grow weary
Or stop from hearing
His voice today.
Today I throw up my hands
Stop shouting commands
Of which I do not deserve.
My hope in life is to always feel You near.
So I wouldn't fear
Or mirror those without Your hope inside.
I don't want to hide.
I wanna flow with the tide of which You have for me.

January 31, 2001

I was inspired by a letter Holly and I received a few
days ago from two sisters that were on the New Jer-
sey Quest trip at our camp ground. They wrote that
the verse they were studying the week they were at the
camp had been 2 Timothy 4:7—"I have fought the good
fight, I have finished the race, I have kept the faith."

February 24, 2001

> *I want my life to speak of You.*
> *Not the sins my heart pursues.*
> *Cleanse me from these hidden desires,*
> *Keep me from deliberate fires!*
> *Don't let them control me.*
> *Then I will be guilt free*
> *And innocent of all sin raging in me.*

March 14, 2001

> *Today I am grateful for the Lord's strength. Sometimes I feel strong, and I know it's from You, Lord. He is the lifter of my head.*

> *Scott, Emma wanted me to tell you "hi" from her mommy, herself, and her grandma and grandpa Nesbitt. And she was blowing spitting noises with her mouth and staring at herself in the mirror. She is so beautiful!*

June 17, 2001

> *Lord, it's Father's Day; comfort the fatherless.*

June 27, 2001

> *My heart aches for other widows or those with pain from loss. When I see them hurting, my heart beats so hard within me and prayers flow for them. But I know how wonderful You are at comforting, and I'm put at ease.*

The LORD will surely comfort Zion and will look with compassion on all her ruins; he will make her deserts like Eden, her wastelands like the garden of the LORD. Joy and gladness will be found in her, thanksgiving and the sound of singing.

Isaiah 51:3 (NIV)

❧ *Holly*

Emma slept with me, for it was comforting to have her near me. I would fall asleep to the sound of her sucking on her binkie and feeling her fingers in my hair. Heather's room light was often on; she was always reading her Bible and writing in her journal. Night after night she would bear her soul on those tear-streaked pages. Many times the next day she would read to me what the Lord was teaching her and showing her through Scripture. We marveled at how God was speaking to her—to us. She had such a beautiful way of expressing her heart on paper.

One day when I was alone cleaning the house, I had some Hillsong cranked on our stereo; I was boppin' around, enjoying myself with a feather duster in my hand. The song "This is How We Overcome"[6] came on. These are the words I heard:

> *Your light broke through my night*
> *Restored exceeding joy*
> *Your grace fell like the rain*
> *And made this desert live*
> *You have turned my mourning into dancing*
> *You have turned my sorrow into joy*

Your hand lifted me up
I stand on higher ground
Your praise rose in my heart
And made this valley sing.

I started dancing alone in that room like I had never danced before. I was singing at the top of my lungs, declaring that He had turned my mourning into dancing and my sorrow into joy. He brought rain to my desert and caused me to sing. I felt like I was up on a mountaintop, closer to Him than I had ever been. But then a tear fell from my cheek, and that single tear opened the flood gates as I fell to my knees, weeping out of joy and weeping out of fulfillment in Him. I couldn't tell Him I loved Him enough. He was healing me. I could feel Him rejoicing over me. Our spirits danced together that day!

Living in His Kingdom

LIFE—
THE END OF THE WORLD AS WE KNOW IT!

For just as the Father raises the dead and gives them life, even so the Son also gives life to whom he wishes.

John 5:21 (NASB)

I Am the Way, the Truth, and the Life.

John 14:6 (NASB)

For you have died, and your life is hidden with Christ in God.

Col. 3:3 (NASB)

June 11, 2001

*I've had a hundred emotions today. This morning
I felt depressed. I almost had to force myself to take
a shower.*

Heather

I am amazed at how quickly you can feel like giving up.
One day you're enjoying the pleasures of your days, and
the next you want nothing to do with life. You wonder
if you will ever truly laugh again, and you struggle to
find joy in life.

You care nothing about what's going on in the world
around you, and you wonder why everyone is so consumed with unimportant things! I'm sure some people
thought I was crazy, but I was ready to go home—not
back to my mom's house or back to my old life but
to my real home, the home I read about in Matthew,
Mark, Luke, and John. I wanted to get on with it! My
eyes had been opened.

Remember the scene in *The Matrix* when Neo
(Keanu Reeves) swallows the red pill, and his eyes are
opened to the fact that his life as he knew it was not
real? He had been living in a matrix. Like Neo, I felt
like I'd swallowed a ginormous red truth-pill, my eyes
had been opened, and my life was anything but real.
I had always heard preachers stand behind their pul-
pits and adamantly proclaim that this world is fleet-
ing—here today, gone tomorrow. They'd quote Scripture that says life is but a breath or a mist or a "wind

that passes through and does not return" (Psalm 78:39). But until someone you love becomes that wind that passes through, I don't think you really get the gravity of such a concept. I mean you know it, but you don't live like you know it, which makes me wonder if you really knew it in the first place. You go on with your day, consumed with living life to the fullest, and you almost forget about the possibility of leaving.

Donald Miller, one of my favorite authors, wrote a book titled *Searching for God Knows What*. In it he writes candidly on our need to break the cycle of believing there are formulas to God and doing church and living life. We think that if we follow a well-thought-out plan, we will experience life. When I think about my past, my formula for living was in the list I carried with me for so long: You are born. You grow up and mature. You make mistakes, but you learn from them. Maybe you graduate from high school and move on to college and a career. You go to church once a week and read your Bible and pray daily. You meet the love of your life and maybe throw in a few children. This same process begins for your little ones, and you follow the rules and guide them with the knowledge that you've acquired over the years. You work until retirement and hope that you'll live long enough to experience everything life has to offer. As a grand finale, you die richly blessed. Somehow all this equals a truly good life; but what happens when the formula that you are living by—that others, mind you, have followed and have succeeded with—abruptly brings you to a halt before you reach the all-satisfying end? Have you not added or subtracted correctly?

My life formula disappointed and disillusioned me, and for the first time, I really understood that life comes with no guarantees and that no formula comes pain free. I honestly should have learned that lesson years before, but I only had glimpses of it: children, teens, and parents who died before their time didn't deserve what had happened to them. I had walked around feeling quite indestructible until my invincible shell was brought to contest and reality hit me square between the eyes. From that moment, I struggled with life—with living. I began to understand that I was blowing through this life. I was tired of playing the game. If earth was not my home, why continue living and buying into the world's seductions over and over again?

I sounded suicidal, but I wasn't. I was frustrated— frustrated that I had to go through all of this here on earth when it wasn't my home. Like I said, I wanted to be done with the game. I wanted to be with my God and my loved ones in heaven where we were consumed with Him and in complete peace. Being in the world and not of it? I didn't even want to be in it anymore! Television drove me crazy. The news drove me insane. And if I had to watch one more person throw away his or her frail life to jealousy, anger, self-pity, and ignorance, I was going to have a meltdown! A few times, I did. I threw the remote and pounded on a couch pillow or whatever or whoever was nearby (sorry, Holly). And people in commercials who complained because they didn't know which laundry detergent to use drove me nuts! What a dilemma! I wanted to scream (and maybe I would have if they could have heard me through the TV), "Do you really think that matters in the big scheme of things? Give me a break!"

At this point, my family had grown used to my fixation on heaven, but others had not. One night after church, about five months after the accident, Holly and I went to dinner with some people our own age, and as we sat at Yen Ching sharing some crab rangoon with our new friends, one guy asked a fair question, "What's next? Do you have any dreams or desires?" Maybe he wanted to help us get on our feet, or maybe he was making sure we had a plan and were not simply at home all the time watching soap operas and feeling sorry for ourselves. It was a reasonable question, but I don't believe my response was what they were expecting.

"I hope God comes back tomorrow." It was the first thing that came to my mind, but I could tell it freaked him out a little bit. He might have thought I was depressed or ready to take matters into my own hands, but I wasn't. I genuinely wanted to be home. I was tired and broken, and I wanted to truly be at rest. For the average person, thinking about going home all the time is not normal, so looking back, I see why he looked like he just heard me say that I hated my grandma or I wanted to punch a baby. Our conversation ended abruptly, and I don't think he asked me anything the rest of the night. Maybe he was afraid of what else I might say or of what I might do with my fork.

HOME

God wanted me to long for home, but most of all, He wanted me to *find* home. Finding home seems to be a strange and bizarre concept. How do we find home? Don't we know exactly where home is? Sometimes I feel stuck here on earth. I want to go home, but I can't. His declaration of being I AM challenges me and changes my small perspective. How can I grasp the grand statement of I AM—that He is everything we are looking for? He was asking me to find Him—to find Him to be what I was looking for—right then and there. He wanted me to find my home *in* Him. He wanted to show me how to be in the matrix yet live—living on this earth here and now, yet not simply taking in breath just to get by but living life to the fullest until the day He takes me home.

Scripture uses the word "life" many times, but the most prominent usage to me is when Jesus calls Himself "Life." He said, "I Am the Way, the Truth and the Life" (John 14:6). Jesus brought this to our attention for a reason. Not only does He want us to step into heaven to finally take in the color of His eyes and experience the grand tour of our brilliant mansions and walk along the crystal sea, accompanied by those who have gone on ahead of us. He also wants us to experience life *now*. He wants us to understand that He is worth living for, and He doesn't want us to play the game of life either. He wants to be the reason we wake up in the morning. He wants to be the joy we find in our mundane tasks at hand. He wants to be the laughter among friends over a silly movie. He wants to be our reason for living. As my friend and one of my pastors, Ken Lumley, relentlessly rants and raves, "He wants to *be* our life!"

Rick Warren's *The Purpose-Driven Life,* a bestseller that resonated with so many, focuses on this very subject. It pleads with the man or woman who is ignorantly walking through the motions every day, and it says, "Have life!" Live a life worthy of something—better yet, of Someone. Find out whom you were made *for* and awake. Arise with a reason to breathe in your next breath. God was saying, "Heather, sweetie, I'm really glad you want to be with Me. I'm flattered. I want you to want to be with Me, but I need you to see that this eternity with Me starts now."

I was so consumed with going home that I forgot about living. Eternity isn't a place. It is time. It is forever. When Christ says that He desires us to be with Him for eternity, He means it. When does eternity start? It doesn't just start the moment we take our last breath here on this earth; it starts when we allow Him to be our lives. Eternity with Him begins *now.* If His promises are true—and I believe they are—then He says that He will never leave us, and He'll never abandon us, forsake us, leave us for dead, or reject us. He is now and forever with us.

For so many years, my head had been addicted to earthly desires and dreams with little to no thought about heaven; but as my world—my kingdom—collided with His, I couldn't get my head out of the clouds. I was missing the point! He wanted me to experience life. He wanted me to be like Paul, "For to me, to live is Christ and to die is gain" (Philippians 1:21). Yes, He wanted me to die, maybe not physically (yet), but all together, He wanted me to die. A death to this world, to my desires, and my flesh, but He didn't want me to stay dead. He wanted me to arise, wake from the dead, and live the resurrected life. He wanted me to understand that until He takes me to be with Him face-to-face, I have an invitation to experience life on earth. I may have sounded crazy, but I wasn't going crazy; Paul felt it too: "But I am hard-pressed from both directions, having the desire to depart and be with Christ, for that is very much better; yet to remain on in the flesh is more necessary for Your sake" (Philippians 1:23–24).

I had to get a picture of heaven—my home—and let God transform those images into a ready seed and allow Him to plant it deep within my heart. I had to let it grow and let the desire to be face-to-face with my Savior drive me to jump when I had no strength, climb when the walls looked too high, and shout when nothing in me knew how to speak or what to say. He wanted to set eternity deep in my heart so it would not be the root of my living or a distraction from the here and now.

Not long after the accident, I visited the Brills. We discussed eternity and heaven and spent many hours wondering and longing for them together. Jim is brilliant when it comes to Scripture on things to come; something in how he explains John's revelation and how he leads you through the depths of His Word confirms this gift. One evening we talked all through dinner and then speculated timing and prophecy until almost midnight. I so longed to hear the trumpet blast that I imagined it. I'm speaking literally here. That night when I laid my head down to sleep, I heard it! It felt so real—like I was aware of it rumbling deep within my bones. I thought, "This is it! God, I can't wait to see You. Heaven, here I come!" But after I sat in the stillness of that dark room, with no lift-off, no thrust into the heavens, I realized I had imagined the whole thing. The room seemed a little emptier than before.

God must have some good laughs over me from time to time. Let's get honest—daily. He has been patient with me, and I am thankful. Today I can see why He hasn't rescued me from this matrix and taken me home. Tomorrow may be a different story, but for today, I'm here, and I need to grasp life. If He wants to be my life, then life is worth living; and if He is going to be in the very steps I've yet to take, then I'm not done living. He is my life whether or not my earthly body is underground. He has eternity set on my heart, and I'm thankful to be experiencing life with Him.

January 2, 2002

> *I am driven by the thought that He knows what He wants of me on this earth; as I put one foot in front of the other, He reveals His plan to me.*

ETERNAL LIFE

Before Jesus was arrested, He prayed a prayer in front of His disciples. He prayed for His followers present and those to come, and He prayed that we would receive what had been given to the Son—eternal life. He spells it out completely for us: "This is eternal life that they may know You, the only true God, and Jesus Christ whom You have sent" (John 17:3). So as I understand eternal life, it isn't picking out the décor in your beautiful new mansion to go with the streets of gold that run along the crystal sea. He obviously wants us to comprehend that this eternal life is knowing God the Father, God the Son, and God the Holy Spirit.

Eternal life is not merely eternity in heaven; it is the gracious, wonderful gift of knowing God the Father because He sent His precious Son to earth to show us the face of our invisible God. Because simply knowing God is eternal life, the gift is much more relational and less physical. He didn't say it is knowledge *of* him; He said it is *knowing* him and retraining our thinking and allowing God to show us how we can know Him and His Son—that is the challenge. For too long we've walked down the aisle and prayed a "magic" prayer that gets us into heaven when we die; then we get up from our knees and step right into who we once were, never dying to our old lives.

There is no rebirth, and there is no understanding that we have eternal life at the tip of our fingertips. We simply breathe a sigh of relief and say to ourselves, "Whew! Glad I prayed that prayer. Now I got my ticket to heaven." And God is saddened. We didn't take hold of our gift. Timothy says, "Fight the good fight of faith; *take hold* of the eternal life to which you were called, and you made the good confession in the presence of many witnesses" (1 Timothy 6:12, emphasis added). Has He not asked us to take hold of eternal life—the gift of *knowing* God and His Son? His cry is to those who have stood before many and confessed in believing in the Way, the Truth, *and* the Life. He doesn't want you to miss the Life! You've found the way, you've believed the truth, but live the life that He has for you!

Now choose life … for the Lord is your life.

Deuteronomy 30:19–20 (NIV)

ADDICTION—
THE ART OF LOVING

Get rid of all the vile things that you've become
addicted to ... I alone am God, your God.

Ezekiel 20:7 (MSG)

And you shall love the LORD your God with all
your heart, and with all your soul, and with all your
mind, and with all your strength.

Mark 12:30 (NASB)

Throw out a word like addiction, and many times we
get a negative taste in our mouths. What does addiction have to do with anything godly? Not long ago,
someone told me that I have an addictive personality.

I think it had to do with how many sweets I'd had that day or how I love to pluck hairs, and admittedly, I am addicted to both. I planned to eat one cookie, but I didn't even notice when I picked up another. I realized this when someone pointed at me and laughed as a half-eaten cookie hung out of my mouth. I'm the same with little hairs. When I see one that needs to be done away with, I can't help myself. I will search, turning on all kinds of lights just to see if I've missed one. I tried plucking my legs one day. It's a good thing it hurt too bad to continue because I would have wasted an entire week scouting out those little scoundrels.

One day I had a conversation with a man who came to touch up the paint in my house, and I don't know exactly how we got on the conversation, but after a bit of sharing, Mark told me that he had been through some heavy addictions—mostly alcohol. He had gone through the AA program and is now watching his children battle addiction as well.

I confessed, "I've been told I have an addictive personality and that it's been a good thing that I've never been around some of those things long enough to gather an appetite for them; although, I can see how quickly it could happen." I wasn't trying to make light of his struggles by any means, but I said, "Addiction is not all bad, though." He was confused. "Yeah, I like sugar too much, but my addiction—the thing that consumes me—is God. I guess at some level we were made for something else to fill us, and we just keep looking in all the wrong places. Depending on the thing we choose, those addictions will determine the consequences that follow." If I let it, my sugar addiction will lead to obesity, heart problems, and at some point, death. My plucking fixation, if I let it consume me, will lead to a nickname Heather-No-Brow; and at some point, my baldness—simply because I'm a tweezer enthusiast.

Since I'm confessing, here's another addiction of mine. I'm kind of embarrassed to go here right after I shared my total fixation on heaven, but I guess this will just explain the roller-coaster ride I found myself on most days. A few months after the accident, Holly and I became consumed with the Gap. Part of the problem was that we were bored, and their sale racks were pretty incredible. But we were also hurting, and shopping for new clothes made us feel a little less miserable. It was fun for a while—really fun—but there was a moment when it just made me sick.

First of all, the clerks knew us by name: red flag number one. Second, a sickening feeling came over me in the middle of a loaded trip to the dressing room, not joy. Shopping wasn't making me feel good anymore, and I came to a point where I didn't want to buy anything: I didn't even want to go to the mall or look at another magazine. The thought of shopping just left me empty. It was unsatisfying, and I didn't want it anymore. I'm thankful for those moments in our lives, because that's when we come to a crossroad. God doesn't want us to learn the hard way, because it kills Him to see us prostituting ourselves out there like that; at the same time, He gives us over to those things, so we can see that we are really looking for Him.

However, my short love affair with the Gap led

me to see that I had been looking for God among the clothing racks. When I slipped on my new baby-blue shirt, I was really looking for the love and acceptance and attention that He alone could give me. I was trying to buy happiness. Standing at my crossroads, I said to God, "I know that road doesn't lead to You; what I'm looking for is You." I turned my affection to the One who truly deserved it, and as I began to be consumed with Him, His voice, His touch, and His words, I was truly satisfied like never before.

DEPENDENCE

I guess this idea of being addicted to God isn't as life threatening as one might expect—or is it? *Addiction* refers to a dependence on something. The definition states that it is "a state of physiological or psychological reliance on a drug liable to have a damaging effect." Yep, that's how I felt. I was dependent and consumed with God, and He was for sure doing some damage. When I think of an addict, I think of being a slave to something; the one addicted may make the choice to partake at first, but at some point there is an exchange of power, and in a moment, that very thing has its grip on the addict. It's funny that Scripture speaks of taking hold, when the exact opposite begins to take place; as you take hold of Him, He takes hold of you.

This journey of taking hold led to my addiction. In my desperation to find Him and know Him, I fell into His grip, and I became madly in love with Him. I emphasize madly. Addictions drive you mad, and this madness is what presses us to experience life and the intimacy He promises. I felt like the woman in the Bible who, while Jesus was passing by in a crowd, thought to herself, "If only I could grab the hem of His garment, I would be healed!" She knew something then that changed her life forever; she knew she must take hold of Him. I know what will save my life—what will bring me healing day in and day out: grabbing onto Him.

Some addictions have led many down roads of pain and destruction: the alcoholic who is fixated on getting his or her next drink and ends up on the street with no job, no money, and no desire for friends and family; the drug addict who is obsessed with a temporal high and hides away in his house, letting the world go by; the gambling addict who waits hour after hour for a moment of glory that will earn back half of what has been lost; and the shoplifter who can't keep her hands from taking just one more item off the rack. Desperate. Addicted. Slaves.

I can't explain away these actions, but I can relate. At some level, I understand and find these responses a distorted picture of our need for Christ. In all my examples, I hear them saying, "I am going to give myself away over and over again until I get what I'm looking for." You've heard it said that we are born with an emptiness in our souls—a God-sized hole that can only be filled by God Himself. Much like a raging alcoholic, we seek to quench our thirsts and fill our cups over and over again, but we are left dry, parched, and longing for more. So we try again and again and again.

Sometimes the alcohol gives us pleasure for a fraction of a second, and because it gave us some satisfaction we think maybe we just need more.

For some, TV is their drug of choice, taking us to another place and numbing our pain for a few hours. What happens when we're addicted to our spouse or our kids? We make them the object of our affection, but when they can't fill up that hole, we try to make it work by seeking more time, squeezing out more affection and twisted ambition, and suffocating the life right out of our relationships. We leave the innocent bystanders we love maimed and scarred because of our search for self-fulfillment. What happens when we stumble upon Jesus? What happens when we come face-to-face with the Trinity?

Over these last few years, I've been confronted with Jesus and who He really is, not the make-believe Christ I had always conjured Him to be—the kind of god that made me feel good and in control. In *this* encounter with the *real* thing, I have found myself drawn to Him. How he dealt with others in the gospels is how He deals with me today. When I read how He rescued Paul, how He cried with Mary, how He stormed through the temple, or how He said, "Let the children come to Me," I know He is real. The authenticity in His demeanor silences my doubts. He speaks truth, and whether or not it's painful, it's always what needs to be said.

At the beginning of this book, I wrote about coming face-to-face with Him and wondering if I had ever truly known Him before. I wonder if we get caught up in pasting our dream Jesus together like girls do with their dream guy. We throw in some charm, great hair, and a smile that lights up a room, and we say, "Voilà!" At some point the thrill runs out, and we're left wondering why this Jesus thing didn't work or why He never became everything that others promised Him to be. I wonder if it's because we didn't really encounter Him. We never got a real good look at His face. We never got a genuine taste of Him. I wonder if we are left unsatisfied because we didn't really meet Him and take in the person of Christ.

I once had a tamed religion. On the peripheral, there were some unknowns, but I chose not to go anywhere if it made me too uncomfortable. If He doesn't make you a bit uncomfortable, maybe you aren't looking directly at Him. I say "uncomfortable," and I mean that, but there's an attraction mingled with this discomfort. It's what makes Him down right enticing. In the core of who you are, you know He's truth, and this truth brings parts of you alive. He never intended to scare you off; although for some, that's their response. Encountering Christ, whether it's your first time or your hundredth time, is cause for a response. And this response comes with a cost each and every time.

The rich young ruler encountered the real person of Christ (Luke 18:18–23) but chose to follow his own religion, which was comfortable and made more sense to him and didn't require him to give up his first love—his wealth. We are all addicts. We were made for an addiction—an art of loving that will neither disappoint nor lead you to another. So from one addict to another, I can now testify I have tasted Him, the real Him, and there's no going back. Nothing has ever been more damaging, more irresistible, more life altering than my dependence on Jesus. So when He passes by, will you turn away like the rich young ruler, sad because your life already supports an addiction, or will you take hold of the hem of His garment because He is your only hope for real satisfaction?

> He feeds on ashes; a deceived heart has turned him aside.
> And he cannot deliver himself, nor say,
> "Is there not a lie in my right hand?"
>
> *Isaiah 44:20*

When Christ—the *true* Christ—becomes your addiction, you are overwhelmed with the fact that He is real and that the one you knew before was merely a hodge-podge of you and of whom you wanted Him to be.

TAKING HOLD

An addiction became a way of life for me—or in a deeper sense, it became a way *to* life. As I searched for the only thing that could fill my emptiness once and for all, He began painting a picture of the life He was offering, and I began to see what was required of me. To know Him—to really see whom it was I was dealing with—caused me to love Him deeper, and when you love someone, you want to please them. Pleasing Him is loving Him and nothing else. It is a request to abandon other loves.

I love security, my rights, self, and my family. We all do. But for me to know Him more—to let God become my life—challenged my love for these things. I wish I could say I was eager to let go of my others, but the task before me was daunting. When my head stayed in the clouds, and when my heart was constantly set on eternity, it was easy for me to live and not care whether I lived or died, whether I had much or little, whether I made a name for myself or not, or whether my family lived or went home to be with the Lord. But when He called me to look and take in the world around me, the battle began. How would I live among the tangible things of this world that called for my attention and summoned my love and choose not to lose my grip on Him?

The Bible is clear; it tells us to not love the world or the things in the world. "If anyone loves the world, the love of the Father is not in him" (1 John 2:15). These bold words cut to my very core. But is God saying that He wants us to become so separated from the world that we can't fulfill his commands to follow Him in sharing His name and spreading His fame? Of course, there has to be an answer in the midst of living this eternal life in the world. We are in the world—there's no doubt about that—but how do we keep our hearts from loving it and not being of it? Some days are easier than others. Some days I can choose to crucify my desires and my security to His will and for His glory; other days I try hard to see that my way of life is met by loving things way too much and not loving Him supremely.

"Taking hold," as He describes it, is precisely what

He wants us to do. To take hold of something gives me a picture of grabbing it with both hands. And not lightly, but with a grip that lets the other know you are not letting go, almost bracing yourself for what may challenge your clutch. Picture an addict. The grip on the addiction speaks volumes of life or death dependence.

Taking hold of God requires a letting go of everything else. We can't survive the twists and turns if we are not holding on with all we've got, but we cannot hold on to both. I've seen it a hundred times; a child is playing with something he shouldn't be, and we offer a switch. We first may tell him, "No, Billy, you can't play with that"; but if his grip remains, and we don't want a screaming fit, we offer a switch. We offer him something that he won't be able to refuse, and he knows that if he wants Cheerios, then he'll have to let go of your remote. He can't have both, and he has to make a decision. We have that same decision to make. If we really want God, we have to let go! When we are pursuing Him, when we are taking hold of this eternal life that He's offering us, there's no room for anything else. We can't hold on to reason. We can't hold on to earthly security. We can't hold on to our loved ones. We can't hold on to our money. We can't hold on to our talents. If we are taking hold of Him, we must let go.

CONQUERING LOVE

Three things will last forever—faith, hope, and love—and the greatest of these is love.

1 Corinthians 13:13 (NLT)

My sense of security went out the window after losing James. As I tried to find my way, the Holy Spirit called me to come and indulge in Him. God wanted to fill my brokenness with His grace and power, and He wanted to protect me from giving myself over to other things. I was vulnerable and extra needy. James had been a stronghold in my life—an addiction that I let fill my emptiness. Any blessing can become an adulterous relationship if we love it more than God, and God knew that I was weak and at risk of turning to an "other" to find some sense of peace.

I don't believe that God took James from me to teach me a lesson, but I do think He wanted to use this opportunity to teach me where my affections should begin and end—with Him. Teaching me to walk in truth rather than continuing in this vicious cycle was on His agenda. He knew my traumatized heart could be conned into believing that other relationships, other family members, other material items, and even emotional responses such as anger, bitterness, or depression would fill my emptiness and make me feel whole.

One day I woke up from a horrible nightmare, and I was immediately down and depressed. I sensed in my heart that I needed to run to Him and cry out to Him, but I didn't want to. Later that day, when I was still low and choosing to cry and remain in my self-pity mode, a good friend called me and invited me to lunch. I declined. It wasn't until that night that I finally broke down and said I needed Him. After the simplicity of our encounter, I felt like a new person. The transformation began on my knees; I tried being angry, feeling sorry for myself, and secluding myself from the rest of the world, but nothing came through like He did. Letting go—why do we make it so hard?

Sometimes giving in and giving myself over scares me. When you know Him, you know He's capable of anything. He's God, and He does what He pleases (Psalm 115:3). "Anything He pleases" means that He's capable of wreaking havoc on life as you know it, but this "anything" has to match up with His character: He is good, perfect, true, right, excellent, holy, and just. He can do no wrong, and that should assure us. But what if it doesn't? And the other question: What else are we holding onto? To know Him assures us of two things: 1) He is everything we need, and 2) Everything He does is right and perfect. How can His allowance of taking away someone you love be perfect, just, and kind? We can't seem to reconcile those feelings, and even when we hear, "His ways are higher than ours, and His thoughts are higher than ours," we struggle to hold onto our rights of having a perfect, glorious, what-I-say-goes kind of life. Trusting Him becomes our issue. We want to trust Him, but maybe we've experienced heart-wrenching pain from His own *pleasing*, and how do we reconcile our pain with His pleasure? For me, knowing that He is capable of anything and that He's demonstrated this in my life caused a panic within me as I released my grip on my life to take hold of Him.

FEAR

Worry, concern, and anxiety can be a daily occurrence inside the walls of our hearts, especially when we've fallen into the hands of a God who has allowed pain and disappointment to write the chapters in our stories. In the allegory *Hinds' Feet on High Places*, we meet the main character Much-Afraid. She has started following the Good Shepherd, and he longs to take her out of the village of Much-Trembling to the High Places. Her struggle begins when he chooses to give her two companions for her endeavor: twin sisters, Sorrow and Suffering. I cried when I first read this book because the Good Shepherd asked Much-Afraid to travel with Sorrow and Suffering. I questioned Him as did Much-Afraid, "Couldn't you have given me Joy and Peace?"

Like Much-Afraid, it's hard to not be fearful of what's to come when we know what could be at stake. One of my favorite people in the world often shares with me her struggle with fear. Lori's honesty about wrestling fear mirrors my fear most days. What-ifs haunt her as she pursues taking hold. She has experienced God giving and taking away, and trusting Him with her future seems foolish at times. Even though Lori knows there's nothing she can do to change or completely know God's plan, she works hard to resign perceived rights raging within her. Here's the ringer: Does she want to love God out of fear of what He's capable of, or out of reverent fear—an awe of Whom it is she is taking hold? Not all fear is bad; God says we should fear Him for who He is. He's not one to mess with, and I'm not talking about fear of meeting Him in a dark alley. That's not what He means when He calls us to fear. Scripture is clear that the beginning of knowledge is fear, so as we strive to take hold—which is the pursuit of knowing—how does fear play a healthy part in our lives?

Fear leads us to either dread or revere life. My fear of what-ifs coming true never stem from an admiration of who He is; they always stem from loving other things too much. Some days Lori takes hold out of fear, hoping that if she holds on, He won't take or hurt the

things that are precious to her. She's striving to protect other loves; she admits it's wrong, and she wants
desperately to take hold out of reverence and as an act
of worship to her Lord. As we talk about her fears of
what might happen, whom He might take, who might
get cancer, and so on, we always come out comforting
one another with *Whom* it is we have been asked to
trust and fear.

We get to trust the heart of our Creator—One
who calls Himself love. Love didn't have to prove anything, yet He proved His perfection and dedication on
an abominable cross. Our sins led Him to His death,
pierced Him for our offenses, crushed Him for our sins,
beat Him to make us whole, and bruised Him for our
healing. Our sins fell on Him that day (Isaiah 53: 4–6).

A man of sorrows, and familiar with suffering.

Isaiah 53:3 (NIV)

But love shows His worthiness in the cross, and everything else points to it.

> *The Shepherd put his hand in his bosom, drew
> something forth, and laid it in the palm of his
> hand. Then he held his hand out toward Much-
> Afraid. "Here is the seed of Love," he said.*
>
> *She bent forward to look then gave a startled
> little cry and drew back. There was indeed a seed
> lying in the palm of his hand, but it was shaped
> exactly like a long, sharply-pointed thorn. Much-
> Afraid had often noticed that the Shepherd's hands
> were scarred and wounded, but now she saw that*

the scar in the palm of the hand held out to her was the exact shape and size of the seed of Love lying beside it.

"The seed looks very sharp," she said shrinkingly. "Won't it hurt if you put it into my heart?"

He answered gently, "It is so sharp that it slips in very quickly. But, Much-Afraid, I have already warned you that Love and Pain go together, for a time at least. If you would know Love, you must know Pain too."[7]

FROM DARKNESS TO LIGHT— A REASON TO SHINE

And God said, "Let there be light," and there was light.

Genesis 1:3 (NIV)

He redeemed my soul from going down to the pit, and I will live to enjoy the light.

Job 33:28 (NIV)

God describes Himself as the great I Am. Even so, I questioned His loyalty, His deliverance, and His promises; and each time, He responded so matter-of-factly,

so personally, and so perfectly. How can He be everything we need—everything we are looking for? He
knew what I needed even before I did, and as I watched
Him work in my life, the change was almost as abrupt
and revealing as stepping from darkness into light.

There's something about being in physical darkness. I don't know if it's true for you, but something
comes over me when I'm lying in the dark; sometimes
it makes me feel uncomfortable and fearful, but other
times the stillness of the moment brings clarity—and
that makes me nervous.

For a time, I despised the night because of the dark,
and part of me, even now, still gets a little uncomfortable with nighttime. I'm fine if it's late, and we're out
and about, possibly walking down a lit street. And I'm
fine if we're camping, as long as we have a good, strong,
campfire to illuminate the faces around me. But I'm
talking about being in total darkness. And I don't think
I'm the only one that feels the dark. Why do most children feel a little more secure with a night-light? Why
do a vast number of Americans fall asleep in front of
their televisions? Aren't they all trying to escape the
darkness? If they are entertained into a deep sleep, they
surpass any uncomfortable moment of stillness and the
heaviness a night can bring.

There's a reason we don't like to be in pitch-black
darkness. I think it's spiritual. Jesus called Himself the
Light for a reason. Has He created physical darkness
just so we would crave the Light? Have you ever stumbled into a dark room? The first thing you seek out
is light. Why? Because it shows us reality, illuminates

what we were looking for, and brings us assurance of where to take the next step. Light gives us confidence.

Many nights I cringed at the thought of lying in the dark, for the darkness illustrated my life. I was in the dark. Everything was crazy and up in the air, and I just begged for answers—light. The stillness of night made my brain run wild. I would be full of conversation and spunk, but when the lights went out, something came over me; in a way, the darkness made me more aware of my need for Him.

Even after seven months, Holly and I still dreaded going to bed. Night's stillness made us uneasy. I was anxious about crawling into bed because I was aware of what was waiting for me: loneliness. I lay there for a while with my eyes open and tried to get comfortable, but I couldn't. To no avail, I tried to still my mind. I felt so alone. Holly had Emma to cuddle, but Holly still felt it too—the darkness.

One night I grabbed all the pillows I could find and tried to create a cocoon to surround me; I wanted to create a feeling of security and confidence. Emotion rushed over me as I thought about my status: widowed, abandoned, deserted, companionless, forgotten. As the darkness rolled in, my tears followed, and I tried really hard for a few brief moments to keep them from beginning their trek down my cheeks. I had been here before: alone with a tear-soaked pillow and my friend hopelessness. Part of me wondered how I could have been so carefree moments ago and now the rollercoaster of emotions caught me by surprise.

But darkness, like I said, can lead us to the Light.

And when you heard the voice *from the midst of the darkness,* while the mountain was burning with fire, you came near to me.

Deuteronomy 5:23 (NIV, emphasis added.)

Once again I found myself in darkness. I was lost. Darkness engrossed me to the point of despair and bitterness, and I needed some light to get me out of my mess. How could I forget? He speaks through the darkness, and I asked God to be who He said He was!

I have come as Light into the world, so that everyone who believes in Me will not remain in darkness.

John 12:46 (NASB)

My grieving heart was trying to call the shots, but I knew that He didn't want me to stay in the dark. I was His, and He was my promise of escaping from the darkness to His marvelous light.

DARKNESS

In Scripture, God used darkness to attack enemies (Joshua 24:7), to illustrate the unknown (Job 12:22), to describe desperation (Job 15:23, 17:12), to portray sin (Ephesians 5:11), and to describe hell (2 Peter 2:9). Darkness is rarely a good thing, and in Scripture we see that God always tried to bring His people out of darkness and into light. For many, the fearful feelings of being in the dark are real. For me, it was real, and it was spiritual.

Darkness hides the truth, and we can find ourselves cowering in a corner, enveloped with thoughts of the unknown, hoping for a glimmer of light. In bed that night, covered by a darkness so thick I could almost feel it, I cried out for my light—my knight in *shining* armor! I told Him what I needed. He already knew. I told Him that I missed my best friend. He responded, "I Am." I said, "I miss my daddy." Again He replied, "Heather, I Am." Through the tears, I managed to whisper, "But what about my husband?" He whispered back, "I Am." Did He answer my Whys? Did He give me direction for tomorrow? No. He knew what I needed; I needed to be rescued from the grave of despair, and I needed to step into His healing light. The truth of His words split open the dark depths of my heart, and He shone His light inside. It was almost too simple, but those two words invaded the darkness and brought me face-to-face with the light.

> What I tell you in the darkness, speak in the light; and what you hear whispered in your ear, proclaim upon the housetops.
>
> *Matt. 10:27 (NASB)*

Anytime God speaks to us, we're not supposed to hold it in. Of course, His word is for us, but His ways are beyond measure. As His children, we are to help reconcile others to Christ—to bring others to Him! To bring them out of the dark to Light! And what God said to me among the shadows was a call to approach the light; I was hopeless, and He became my hope. He whispered words of acceptance and love, and I had to proclaim them "upon the housetops" (Matthew 10:27).

If you aren't seeking opportunities to proclaim His word on the housetops, it's funny how He'll help with that. Holly, Heidi, and I were learning incredible truths about Him, and I believe that the Lord—in His choosing—moved us to our housetops. He gave us a platform to stand on where we could boast about His nearness, His sovereignty, and His goodness, and we found ourselves in front of various churches, worshiping Him in word and in song. Churches would call us and ask if we'd come share our testimonies, and before we knew it we were traveling around together along with some other musicians that went to our church. Some people ask us how it all began, and I can honestly say it had nothing to do with us, and everything to do with His choosing. There's really no other way to explain it. We were not seeking it. We were seeking healing, and our healing—in God's plan—included us speaking and singing on behalf of this light. What He whispered to us in the dark is what He had us bring to light. We worshiped our God in front of others, and God did what He pleased through us.

It sounds unconventional and a little absurd for us to visit churches and say some of the things God led us to say while we were still recovering from the most horrific time in our young lives, but for our own healing and for God's beautiful way of bringing ashes to beauty, we agreed to each and every opportunity. It wasn't always pretty or polished, but it was real and it was how we brought a sacrifice offering to the Lord.

Holly and I wrote lyrics and even some melodies to accompany our expressions, and Heidi joined us in this process. The Lord somewhat kept us blinded to our activities to keep us from going mad, but at the same time He used them to keep us pressing into Him. I caught a glimpse of how He was trumping tragedy, and I loved Him for it. Sometimes these moments of joy chipped away at the heartache; other days they seemed to intensify it.

Before one of our concerts, I stood in a back room, begging God to release me from my responsibility. I wanted to heal on my own terms; I wanted to be secluded so I could work through some of these things silently. Why did my pain have to be so public? I didn't believe that I could tell the story of losing James one more time, and if I tried, I thought I might embarrass myself by running out of the building or by sobbing uncontrollably.

We were going to begin in twenty minutes, but I was about to hyperventilate because of my anxiety and fear. I cried out to God and told Him that if He still wanted to use me, He would have to do it all because I had nothing left. I paced around the room and asked the Holy Spirit to fill me with words and song. Darkness tried to hold me down; obviously our enemy didn't want me to speak this message of reconciliation, hope, or restoration. He wanted to hide what God was doing in our lives, and he wanted to destroy us by reminding us of our inadequacies or of how heavy our hearts still were. His whispers were easy to believe: "God has put you through so much, and now He's subjecting you to such torture by making you re-live those moments over and over again. Everyone thinks you're crazy for sharing so soon. They don't expect you to be ready for something like this, why does He?" There were many days I let him win, but when I remembered how sweet being in the light really felt, I had to hold on to what I had been told: Don't ever doubt in the dark what He's told you in the light. This was truth, and I knew I must cling to God's Word, His promises, and even His whispers. I replaced the lies that I had been listening to with the light of the truth. My battle came to an end when I let the light invade my darkness.

That night God said to me, "'My grace is sufficient for you, for My power is made perfect in weakness.' Therefore I will boast all the more gladly about my weaknesses, so that Christ's power may rest on me" (2 Corinthians 12:9). God's power rested on me, and I had the honor and privilege to speak once more on behalf of His life, His healing, and His nearness.

> For our struggle is not against flesh and blood, but against the rulers, against the powers, against the world forces of this darkness, against the spiritual forces of wickedness in the heavenly places.
>
> *Ephesians 6:12 (NASB)*

That's why the darkness—even physical darkness—feels like a spiritual battle. In the beginning, God saw that the light was "good," and He separated the light from the darkness (Genesis 1:4). They are opposites, and we are either in the light or in the darkness—the two can't exist in the same place at the same time. The same is true with good and evil. God is light, and there is no darkness in Him at all (1 John 1:5); but while we stand in the darkness, He calls to us from the light. At the same time, Satan dresses up in God-like attire and tricks us into believing that he is the light (2 Corinthians 11:14), but Satan is a liar and a manipulator; sometimes the only way he can get us to follow him is by pretending to be the light. When I listened to the enemy's voice telling me those lies, I had to remember what had been revealed to me in the light.

THE SUN

The greatest source of light and energy on earth is the sun, and I love the way the sun makes me feel—like everything must be right in the world. There is no better way to start my morning than by waking up to a burst of sunlight through the window. As long as the sun's shining overhead, I love any season.

Many have tried to explain and calculate the power in the sun, but no one has ever tried to step foot on it because they know that the journey alone would kill them. Even though it's billions of miles away, the sun can still burn my skin in a matter of minutes; this fascinates me.

God describes Himself as the sun, for just as the sun rises every day to lift our souls and provide nourishment for survival, so it is with our God. Daybreak is a physical portrait of light invading darkness. Have you ever watched the sun break through a cold, dark night and been reminded of its powerful beauty? A small blush of color fractures the black sky and begins the dance of brilliance. It ushers in new beginnings and the start of another day, and who can stop it? Every day—from sunrise to sunset—the sun moves in perfect time across the sky. It is never in a hurry. And even when the clouds hide its appearance, the sun is still there.

So, too, when the storms of life or blanketing clouds try to conceal the Lord's face, He still shines. We may not be able to see Him, but we can rest assured that the sun never changes; the only thing that changes is our perspective. I've seen the sun rise in Florida, in Costa Rica, in Missouri, and in Illinois, and every sunrise I've seen has looked a bit different than the others, yet the sun was the same each and every time. God is the same yesterday, today, and forever.

> Arise, shine, for your light has come, and the glory of the Lord rises upon you.
>
> *Isaiah 60:1 (NIV)*

> God made two great lights—the greater light to govern the day and the lesser light to govern the night.
>
> *Genesis 1:16 (NIV)*

> In the same way, let your light shine before men, that they may see your good deeds and praise your Father in heaven.
>
> *Matthew 5:16 (NIV)*

> You are the light of the world. A city on a hill cannot be hidden.
>
> *Matthew 5:14 (NIV)*

While God refers to Himself as the sun, He refers to us as light; and when we encounter Him, we are brought into the sunlight, and we start to shine. Moses shone with the glory of the Lord too. As he stood before I Am on Mount Sinai, God's presence transformed him from the inside out, and when Moses came down the mountain and returned to the Israelites—Ten Commandments in hand—they were "afraid to come near" him (Exodus 34:30). Why? Moses was physically reflecting God's light. Moses didn't even know that his face was glowing!

If God is the sun, who are we? Scriptures refer to us as cities on a hill and lamps to shine where others can see the light, but Louie Giglio was the first teacher I heard describe us as moons. The moon is a simple rock; there's not much to it until the sun shines on it. In her song, "You are the Sun,"[8] Sara Groves sings:

> *You are the sun shining down on everyone*
> *Light of the world giving light to everything I see*
> *Beauty so brilliant I can hardly take it in*
> *And everywhere you are is warmth and light*
> *And I am the moon with no light of my own*
> *Still you have made me to shine*
> *And as I glow in this cold dark night*
> *I know I can't be a light unless I turn my face to you*

If He is the sun, then we are the moon. Moses was the moon, I can be the moon, and you can be the moon when you are looking right at Him. Even without anything to generate this glow on our own, we can shine. "As the glory of the Lord rises upon you," know this:

You are radiating His glory (Isaiah 60:1). Moses radiated the Lord's glory so much that he had to wear a veil over his face after being with God. He was nothing special—just a man with his face turned toward the light.

As moons reflecting brightly, we can only boast in the One shining on us, simple rocks. God can bring about creation and beauty from a little earth and dust, so why are we surprised that He can make a lifeless rock fill the night sky with the sun's light? We are made in His image—made to display our maker—and I want others to look at me and say, "With no light of her own, she shines when her face is turned toward the Son." Sara suggests that we are "cold dark stones," yet the Lord has made us to shine by reflecting His light and His image.

> Then your light will break forth like the dawn, and your healing will quickly appear.
>
> *Isaiah 58:8 (NIV)*

The light walked among us over two thousand years ago. He invaded darkness and took death with Him to the grave. Darkness thought he had won; he celebrated and danced about, believing that he had snuffed out light forever. But light could not be stopped and did not stay under ground; He rose from the grave after three days. Day broke, and once and for all, light put an end to dark's power over death by shining bright and covering the earth.

He asked others to join in His brilliance, and we are now carriers of the light and are called to invade the darkness by bearing the reflection of the one and only pure light. When light comes again and breaks through the night one last time, dark will no longer compete with light: no shadow will hide the day, no storm will conceal the sun, and no cloud will cover the sun's warmth. Light is coming, so let us turn our faces to the Son and shine, holding high the mission of the carrier: reflecting His glorious image.

Holly

We had once dreaded the night, but God changed our hearts, and evening became our sweet time with our Husband. What a dramatic change this was from when we feared the night. Now we longed for it. Heather and I would each go to our rooms after an evening meal and feast upon His Word—listening for His voice. The music in my soul began to sing like never before. My heart would dance when thinking of my time alone with Him. Jesus really became my Lover, my Healer, my Deliverer, my Strong Tower, my Best Friend. No one understood me like Him.

MY HUSBAND—
'TIL DEATH DO US PART

Keep me as the apple of your eye; hide me in the shadow of your wings.

Psalm 17:8 (NIV)

A good name is more desirable than great riches; to be esteemed is better than silver or gold.

Proverbs 22:1 (NIV)

You will forget the shame of your youth and remember no more the reproach of your widowhood. For your Maker is your husband—the Lord Almighty is his name—the Holy One of Israel is your Redeemer.

Isaiah 54:4b-5 (NIV)

The dictionary's definition of grieving is "to experience great sadness" or "distress." A few weeks after I returned to Jefferson City, a friend of mine sent me a small book on the five stages of grief, and I wondered if I would ever make it through these horrible stages. People have spent a great deal of their lives identifying these phases of grief; maybe they want to encourage those who are going through the process that they're not alone. But maybe these psychiatrists have devoted their time to the grieving process to assure the loved ones of the grieving that the grieving are not going crazy. Probably the most well-known book on this topic is Elisabeth Kubler-Ross's book, *On Death and Dying*[9]. In it she identifies five stages that one would go through either if one were diagnosed with a fatal disease or at the loss of a loved one.

- Denial (this isn't *happening* to me!)
- Anger (why is this happening to *me?*)
- Bargaining (I promise I'll be a better person *if…*)
- Depression (I don't *care* anymore)
- Acceptance (*I'm ready* for whatever comes)

For me, these stages played out as I worked through my heartache. Depending on what was happening in my life or whether I was nearing an anniversary, some days I slipped back into one or multiple stages, but my healing required taking a journey through each one. Denial was accompanied by numbness; depression, disorder. But acceptance came. We have to make it through these stages and end on acceptance; if we don't, we live as slaves to pain, hopelessness, bitterness, and sin.

A wedding has not taken place until the vows are made, the commitments are spoken, and the pronouncements are given. You can dress up in your big, white, fancy dress, and the groom can stand in his place next to the pastor. The miniature bride on your cake can look just like you, and the children can steal the show by throwing petals all the way down the aisle. You can walk into the heavily decorated sanctuary surrounded by your friends and family. Your dad can shed a tear as he hands you over to your fiancé. A family member or friend can read Scripture or sing a song. But until the vows are made, no exchange of promise has taken place and no lifelong commitments have been made. Without a vow, all you have is a room full of costumes; there is no union and no marriage.

On June 5, 1999, James and I said our vows and became husband and wife. We made our promises, exchanged our rings, and sealed it with a kiss; but one year later, I watched his casket close and sink into the ground. Our vows seemed left undone. Had I kept up with my end of the bargain? The vows were fresh in my mind, for I was still trying to comprehend the tasks of being a wife. I had just embarked on my journey of being James's partner through thick and thin when all came abruptly to an end as death parted us.

Was I in denial? Yes, I wanted to live there as long as I could. To imagine this was just a dream gave me hope of his return, but denial could only remain alive as long as I was willing to live out a lie. I had to face the reality that Lazarus was not coming out of the tomb this time.

Was I angry? There were days that anger ruled my responses and my mind. The rights that I thought I was entitled to piled up, and I looked upward and said, "How could You let this happen?" Then I looked outward and said, "Life's not fair! James had so much life left to live!"

Did I bargain? Yes; but even as the promises flew off my tongue, I realized I could beg, but God would not rewind the clock and magically take me back to the life I lived before. If He allowed these events to transpire, He wouldn't be changing them.

Was I depressed? For me, depression was the best part of my grieving process. I know that sounds like I'm out of my mind, but once I got to this stage I started healing. In depression, your eyes are solely on yourself, your pain, and your loss, but eventually you get sick of thinking about yourself, and that's when your eyes catch a glimpse of something bigger—something much larger than you. I was done trying to live in the past, and I was through trying to recover what I had lost; I was finally dead.

Dead? Are you wondering how that can be a good thing? My sweet friend, this is the beauty: God can only resurrect dead things! I knew that He wasn't going to bring James back among the living and that He had another plan. He was going to bring *me* back among the living! I may have been breathing in oxygen, but He had life in store for me. My battle with despair led me to my knees, which led me to the cross.

Jesus did something incredible that dark day: He conquered death, which meant He had power over death. Releasing my fear of death and dying, I had to surrender to this power of resurrection—and thus surrender to death of self, to death of dreams, to death of desires, and to death of rights—and submit to His will, all to be resurrected into a new creation. Surrender happens by choice; Jesus made a choice to surrender to what the Father asked of Him, and I needed to do the same. Has He asked you to surrender to the journey of walking in the shadow of the valley of death? It's hard to submit to a request like that, isn't it? We want some way around it, but He beckons us to walk through the valley—not alone, but with Him all the way.

Psalm 23 is probably one of the most well-known and quoted chapters of Scripture in the entire Bible. Why? Maybe because life is full of pain and death. At some point in our lives, it seems that everywhere we turn, someone is dying. If you read the news, if you turn on your local television station, or if you spend any amount of time outside the walls of your home, you hear people dealing with the possibility of or the actual loss of a loved one. People find themselves in this valley every day; they are afraid of it, and they don't want to walk it alone. Even if they don't have a relationship with I Am, these verses calm many grieving hearts, which is probably why segments of this Scripture end up on countless funeral programs. It gives people peace that if their loved ones walked through the valley, the Lord was with them, for they want to believe that their loved ones were not alone. As Christ-followers we are never alone because we have asked Christ to walk with us through the valleys, on the mountaintops, in the deserts, and through the storms. He promises to walk with those who believe in Him, and He must keep His promises, or He'll be a liar. So through the valley I had a companion, and we walked hand in hand.

I cried the first time I went to the grocery store by myself. James and I had lived our lives doing practically everything together. We went to work around the same time, and most days we ate lunch together. He'd pick me up from work, and we'd spend the rest of our evening together; and we typically went grocery shopping together. He had always been with me. As I strolled through the cereal aisle, pain seized my heart, and I started sobbing. I tried to control myself but sometimes you can't tell your tears to stop. I knew everyone thought I was crazy, so I just tried not to make eye contact. I thought about leaving, but I knew I had to learn to do these things without James. I went through the lonely aisles by myself, picking out peanut butter and frozen pizzas by myself. I had no idea that a simple trip to the grocery store could make me feel so alone.

The grocery store had been a valley, but was I truly alone? No; God was there as I picked up my box of Frosted Shredded Wheat. He was there when my eyes were so clouded with tears that I couldn't read the nutrition label on a box of cookies. "Even though I walk through the valley of the shadow of death, I fear no evil for You are with me" (Psalm 23:4). What possibly could be evil in the middle of Walmart? Bitterness, anger, and hopelessness were always prowling about, waiting for weak moments. Their goal was to attack and leave me for dead, but they could not get their hold on me because my Protector was there, walking with me, comforting me, and asking me to take hold of Him. There's no shame in crying when we're in our valleys, for sometimes all we can do is hold on tight with one hand to our Savior and one hand to our tissues.

As I said earlier, my depression led to death, but death led to resurrection! What if the valley of the shadow of death is less about surviving it and more about us ending up dead? What if that's how He uses those valleys? Can you picture it? He leads us through plush green pastures, along quiet waters, and down paths that escort us to restoration and refreshment before arriving to a place of honor where others praise His name for all that He's done in us. We experience these heights—almost giving us a sneak preview of things to come—and then so quickly we find ourselves walking the road to death with enemies surrounding us, calling out for us to turn and run and trying to convince us that the Lord is not to be trusted. Selfishness, bitterness, and fear call our names, but He protects us with His own rod and staff. He hasn't led us here to desert us; He wants us to see something about Him. Paul called it "dying daily" (1 Corinthians 15:31) but maybe this begins by walking through the valley of the shadow of death and by fearing no evil, no enemy, no past, and no desire. He wants us to see that the road to death leads to real living.

When all is right in the world, we find it easy to love God, but when we are in the valleys we find it harder to convince ourselves that He's good. We find it harder to trust, to love, and to give ourselves over to His pleasing. As I walked through the valley, He was leading me to my death—death of self, of my selfish will, and of my rights to a controlled and enjoyable life. My concept of life looked a lot different than this dark valley, and the old me stood opposing this journey, but I couldn't let her win. I had to walk through this shadow of death to be made alive. At the end of that small chapter, you hear resurrection in David's voice, "Your beauty and love chase after me every day of my life. I'm back home in the house of God for the rest of my life" (Psalm 23:6 MSG). Home—making our home with Christ.

AT HOME WITH A NEW NAME

Though I had only been married for a year, I wanted to keep his name, and I wanted to wear my ring. I wanted to know that I still belonged to James. I was his girl. This caused some awkward moments. Strangers would ask how long I had been married, and when you're out of the denial stage and into the depression stage, you might stumble over your words, but you end up telling them like it is, which is not generally a conversation builder but rather a conversation disaster. No one expected it. It was like asking a woman how far along she is and then finding out she isn't pregnant. By wearing my wedding ring, I was asking for it, but I didn't know what else to do. Taking it off made me feel worse.

The night I described earlier—while lying in the dark, asking God to be everything that He promised to be—was a night that brought about revelation and comfort beyond words. His response was an all-encompassing, "I Am." What a loaded answer indeed! I hadn't felt alone in a long time. At the end of high school and early in college, I had dated a guy for two years, and as the Lord brought that relationship to an end, James showed up. I had learned how to live by always turning to that other person, so when God spoke in the dark that night regarding my desire for my husband, He was speaking to much more.

> You will forget the shame of your youth and remember no more the reproach of your widowhood. For your Maker is your husband—the Lord Almighty is his name—the Holy One of Israel is your Redeemer.
>
> *Isaiah 54:4b-5 (NIV)*

Singleness was one of the greatest gifts the Lord could have given me. I met my Husband, and as He introduced me to I Am, I saw a pattern emerging. It is my prayer that you've already caught a glimpse of this pattern through the pages of this book.

> In the year of King Uzziah's death, I saw the Lord.
>
> *Isaiah 6:1 (NAS)*

When I lost everything, I finally came face-to-face with the Lord, with I Am. He revealed Himself to me only when my eyes failed to see anything else but Him and when I finally locked eyes with His. For me, this encounter took place amid dust and ashes. I don't know what ashes you stand on or what pain has brought you to this book, but I pray that your eyes have locked with His. He wants us to know what I Am truly means. His name alone is Life. His name alone is Love. His name alone is Light. In the dark that lonely night, He called Himself my Husband alone. Only during my single years was I able to see this name come to mean Ultimate Companion.

I was a widow. A stigma went with that word, and I made more jokes about myself as a widow, sometimes to push away the feelings that went along with this reminder. I had always thought of older women dealing with this label, not a woman in her twenties! But the Lord spoke directly to my heart on this subject. Not only are widows mentioned in the Bible, they have God's attention. He said a demonstration of pure and lasting religion is "caring for orphans and widows in their troubles" (James 1:27). I was fatherless *and* husbandless, but God wasn't done writing His story for my life; He wanted me to know how He felt about me. The Word made it clear that He is about protecting the widow (Proverbs 15:25), that He gives honor to the widow (1 Timothy 5:3), that He asks others to plead for the widow (Isaiah 1:17), and that He is not above using widows to fulfill His purposes (1 Kings 17:9). Even though I hated the name, I felt special, as if He was singling me out. He had His eye on me. Anytime I read Scripture and saw my name—widow—a sharp thorn pierced my heart, but He covered the wound with words of affirmation and love.

Of course, He's all about changing us—even our names. God changed Abram's name when he said, "No longer shall your name be called Abram, but your name shall be Abraham; for I will make you the father of a multitude of nations" (Genesis 17:5). Jacob, which means liar, cheat, and swindler, was changed to Israel after he spent the night wrestling with God. And Paul was once Saul, a name change that represented a change in heart; the Lord gave him a new identity in Christ. Jabez struggled with the meaning of his name: pain. Due to the pain he caused her during childbirth, his mother gave him his name, but he didn't want to live under that label anymore. Me? I needed a new name, for God wanted for me to "forget the shame of (my) youth and remember no more the reproach of (my) widowhood." He declared, "For your Maker is your husband—the Lord Almighty is His name—the Holy One of Israel is your Redeemer" (Isaiah 54:4b-5 NIV). I no longer needed to live under my humility; I had a choice to step into a relationship with God.

A year had come and gone, and when Aaron Snell stepped into our lives, Holly and I experienced an answer to prayer. No doubt we missed our husbands, but we particularly missed male friendship. We missed the dynamics of it. Aaron joined our band, and we immediately connected with him, for his personality and friendship made us smile and added much-needed laughter to our days. He called us his Widow Ministry, and we joked that he was racking up some major points with God each time he came over. How could we have known that Aaron would one day be more than a good friend but also Holly's husband and Emma's daddy! Soon our threesome turned into a two-some. They were both passionate about the same things, and their hearts were both drawn to leading others to worship. Before they knew it, they were falling in love.

Holly

Aaron would come to practice and then linger with Heather and I after practice at our house. We would sit and watch TV, eat leftovers, and laugh until we realized we had to get some sleep. Aaron was just twenty years old, but his young and energetic spirit was so refreshing. He became such a good friend to Heather and me. He began leaving his keyboard at our house, and I can recall many nights when we would head downstairs again with an old hymnal or chorus book and sing and worship together. He would play, and Heather and I would sing. Eventually, Heather and I shared more about our loss and the new journey the Lord had us on, and he sat and listened and lent a sympathetic ear. The comfort these special times brought were so precious to us.

I'll never forget when Aaron told Heather and me how he had seen a television story on us the year before. He was a college student at the time, and it was the only ten o'clock evening news broadcast he had seen all year. His heart was so moved and so grieved, he called his parents late that night to tell them the story. In fact, he called again the very next day, still upset about hearing about two young Christian men killed with wives who were sisters left to pick up the pieces.

As our friendship continued, he started showing up a lot more. He and I began running together in the evenings, going to the golf range, or grabbing a quick bite to eat. Aaron worked at the mall during the day selling shoes at Dillards, so if we didn't see him in the evening for some reason, we would certainly catch him at work as we took our daily shopping trip to the mall. Sometimes he would help us around the house a little if it didn't require too much of a handy-man, but mostly he was just always around. Aaron and I also shared the same passion for leading worship, and many times he would bring whatever worship videos from various churches that he had to our house, and we would sit and watch them together.

A couple of months passed, and I was stunned by the feelings that I began developing for Aaron. I tried to ignore them for a while, but they persisted. I was absolutely disgusted with myself. How could I have feelings for another man when I was still mourning and grieving the loss of my dear husband? Were these types of feelings even possible so soon? What kind of person did that make me?

Regardless of my efforts, Heather and others began to see a change in me. I tried to hide it from them, but it became more and more obvious. Despite my feelings, I knew there was no way that he could possibly be interested in me, and I didn't dare tell him how I was feeling—he was becoming my best friend. That was the one thing I couldn't risk losing. I was a widow, I was six years older than he was, *and* I had a child. He had so much ahead of him. I would only be a burden with major baggage, so I continued to suppress my feelings. I couldn't lose his friendship.

Do you ever have those moments where you're in the middle of such a mundane task and find yourself surprised by the still, small voice of God in your spirit—whispering to you, calling your name? I had one of these moments while I was crying over some potato salad I was making one day. I asked God to forgive me for these feelings I had for Aaron; I felt foolish and so unworthy to even be contemplating having something more with him, but I'll never forget God's voice that day. He simply asked, *Don't you think I want the absolute best for you and for Emma? Trust Me. My child, I will provide the best for you and Emma. Rest in Me.*

> "For I know the plans I have for you," says the Lord. "They are plans for good and not for disaster, to give you a future and a hope."
>
> *Jeremiah 29:11 (NLT)*

After a couple months with my feelings all over the place, the time came for me to tell Aaron how I was feeling. (Plus, I was driving Heather crazy!) I called Aaron on the phone—I couldn't dare talk to him about this in person. I wouldn't be able to handle the rejection on his face. Through tears, I began to share with him my feelings. He was completely silent on the phone. I couldn't tell what he was thinking. It was driving me crazy! He was giving me nothing! His silence caused me to cry a little harder. He then released me of the mounting pressure and softly said, "Holly, I've been fighting the same feelings for months as well. I couldn't ask out a girl who had just lost her husband the past year. I didn't think you would desire someone younger than yourself with less life experience. What do I possibly have to offer you?" I couldn't believe my ears. We got off the phone, and I thought I would pass out from such happiness, but what now? Were we dating? Should I call him my boyfriend? What do we do now?

The Lord really began to help us process our feelings. We knew early on that we could see God's hand in bringing us together for long term. We couldn't fully explain it, and it sure didn't make sense to almost anyone, but we had such a peace about our new relationship. We found a lot of time to continue to be together including Emma. Life was becoming more free, even fun!

Aaron proposed to me on our first "official" date. A few days following the proposal, we then drove to Springfield, Missouri, with Emma to share the news with his family. We had a two-and-a-half-hour drive ahead of us, and my stomach was in major knots. Aaron is the baby in the family, and I knew they had such high hopes for him. I couldn't imagine them being too excited about our news. I wasn't the "ideal" package. I had met Aaron's mom, dad, and sister before, but I had not yet met his brother who lived in Houston, Texas. His parents had made such an impression on me when meeting them before; they were involved in full-time ministry running a type of half-way house for men just out of prison or as an alternative to prison. They were amazing people. I'll never forget the very first time

Emma met Aaron's parents, Jim and Peggy. Aaron took us to their work and introduced Emma to Peggy. Peggy leaning over with the sweetest tone in her voice said, "Emma, it is so nice to meet you." Emma responded by giving her a scowl, kicking her in the shin, and retorting, "You're stupid!"

In spite of my fears, they embraced Emma and me as if we were always meant to be in their family. We hugged and cried together. They even had a big barbecue that night at their house to celebrate our future union.

❧ *Heather*

I struggled with this relationship. I thought it was too soon after losing our husbands for Holly to even consider giving her heart to another. I didn't even know how it could be possible. But as things made their shift, God used that relationship to speak to my troubled heart. One evening I couldn't take it anymore, and I began crying out to God, speaking out of confusion and frustration, and (if I am being completely honest) clouded by a little anger and resentment. I spent the beginning of my prayer pointing fingers at Holly and questioning her state of mind. After my ranting and raving ceased, and God could get a word in edge-wise, He spoke. "Heather, I know the plans I have for you, and I know the plans I have for Holly."

"But how can she be ready? Isn't it too soon?"

He replied, "What are you really afraid of?"

I was trying to point the finger at everyone else but me, so He shined a light on my exact fear—being alone. Losing your husband is devastating, and watching your sister go through the same thing doubles the pain; but on the flip side, you have each other, and I was scared that this time I was going to be left all alone. But God knew the plans He had for me, and He knew the plans he had for Holly. Who was I to question?

They were married seven months later, and their wedding was a beautiful display of redeeming love. Aaron was Holly's kinsman redeemer, and he stepped into the role of husband and father with such grace and ushered Holly and Emma into his heart and into his hands. Aaron could only accept or reject what God was calling him to, and he chose to obey this path of turning ashes into beauty. Aaron was evidence that God's ways were truly higher than ours.

In my heart, I had made my peace with Holly loving someone else, but I didn't want that for myself. My heart belonged to another, and I feared losing this love; but God, in His amazing way, used an illustration to help me understand. He described it as a mother struggling with having more than one child and gave me this parallel: A mother fears that if she has another that she'll lose love for the first child, but God causes a heart to not lose love, rather it gains *more* love. Through that illustration, even though I had no children of my own, I understood. Even then God was helping me process through this season of my healing.

When Holly took Aaron's last name, she left the reproach of her widowhood, but God hadn't forgotten about me. He wanted to give me a new name as well, and it too would happen by making personal and life-long vows. A group of girlfriends from church and I were just starting a new Bible study by Dee Brestin and Kathy Troccoli called *Falling in Love with Jesus,* and I felt like a sponge ready to soak up everything in His Word. As I opened up the book, little did I know that this study would begin a love relationship of a lifetime. The Scripture surrounding the week was in Isaiah: "As a bridegroom rejoices over his bride, so will your God rejoice over you" (62:5b).

Images of James's face gleaming as I walked down the aisle instantly enlightened me to another face that was glowing, "rejoicing" over my coming; God Himself was taking pleasure over me, His bride. Through that study, God led me into a deep, loving relationship with Him that was the beginning of a lifetime of devotion and submission to Him. Yes, He's our Father, Shepherd, Protector, Provider, Friend, but do we understand that He wants us to enter into a love relationship with Him and come to know Him as a wife knows her husband and as a husband knows his wife? The word God uses to explain the intimacy between husband and wife is the same word He chooses to use when He calls us to *know* Him. The word in Greek is *ginosko.* This intimacy between husband and wife is beyond any other relationship God has given us here on earth, and from that day, I understood what He meant when He told me in the dark, "I Am." He was saying, "I Was, I Am, and I Will Be your husband." He was prompting me, just like He is prompting you, to enter into a covenant of marriage with your Maker, your husband. Do you *ginosko* God?

I made a vow a few months later, very similar to the vow I made to James: "I, Heather, take You, my Maker, to be my Husband, to have and to hold from this day forward, for better or for worse, for richer, for poorer, in sickness and in health, to love and to cherish; from this day forward. And even death will not part us!" I made my vow to love Him no matter what comes, and I no longer lingered in my shame. He changed my name.

> You'll get a brand-new name straight from the mouth of God.
>
> You'll be a stunning crown in the palm of God's hand,
>
> A jeweled gold cup held high in the hand of your God.
>
> No more will anyone call you Rejected, and your country will no more be called Ruined.
>
> You'll be called Hephzibah (My Delight), and your land Beulah (Married),
>
> Because God delights in you and your land will be like a wedding celebration.
>
> *Isaiah 62:3–4 (MSG)*

What is your name? Are you tired of hearing it? Divorced, Forgotten, Unlovable, Abandoned, or Single? Are you desperate for a new name? He has a new name for you; He calls you His Delight, Married, Loveable, Chosen, and Bride. As a bridegroom rejoices over His bride, so it is with our God. He takes great delight in calling us His.

> They will be called the Holy People, the Redeemed
> of the Lord; and you will be called Sought After,
> the City No Longer Deserted.

Isaiah 62:12 (NIV)

He calls us sought after! Is it not a woman's desire to be sought after, pursued? We want to know that we are loved and that someone is fighting for us. May those words capture your heart as they have mine. God's Word tells us that we are noticed, seen, and loved. His sweet words flow out of a heart that's crazy about you. My friend Andrea refers to the Lord as a "player." We laugh because He makes us feel special, and we feel like we're the only one He loves. At the same time, I guess there's enough of God to go around.

For Holly, her world collided with Aaron's, and God offered her a chance to experience an earthly redeemer. For me, He took great delight in teaching me to live solely with the name He had given to me—His name.

> Return to Me, for I have redeemed you.

Isaiah 44:22b (NIV)

MY REDEEMER LIVES—
A REAL-LIFE BOAZ

Forget the former things; do not dwell on the past.
See I am doing a new thing! Now it springs up; do
you not perceive it? I am making a way in the desert
and streams in the wasteland.

Isaiah 43:18–19 (NIV)

February 19, 2002

*My prayer is for You to continue healing my bro-
ken places—You are the only one who can handle
the devastation of my heart. I keep thinking about
how You considered it joy to go to the cross. Joy?
That's hard to swallow.*

March 4, 2002

Shattered dreams teach me the only thing I truly desire and should desire is an encounter with my God. When I turn to Him and feel His love, it's a feeling that encompasses me, and I know that's what I've been searching for all this time. To enjoy You—satisfied by a pleasure, this raging, awakening appetite waiting to be found and nourished.

Four years after losing my father, my husband, and life as I knew it, I found myself in Springfield, Missouri, serving at an amazing church, living life married to my God, doing all I could to live day by day, and following His lead. As a youth associate, I was learning what it meant to give myself away by working with teens in the church's youth group. I had never imagined that my life would take such a turn, but I learned as I went, soaking up the amazing leaders around me and hanging on God's every word. I believed what His Word said about His thoughts being higher than mine, and His ways so much greater than mine. My days were filled with more stretching moments than easy ones, and because of this, I sometimes asked Him if I was in the right place. Each time I begged the question, God was quick to affirm His reasoning and His timing among my doubts. He placed me in circumstances where I had to learn how to teach His Word, how to take on the responsibilities of a shepherding Christ-follower, and most importantly, how to be desperate for His constant presence and power in my life. I quickly realized that each day I needed Him and that I had an amazing role in this often complicated life. If I wanted to make a difference or simply please Him, I had to allow that to occur out of the overflow of my life.

The ring finger on my left hand was empty, but I didn't even notice it anymore. I felt taken, loved, spoken for, and remembered. I don't want to imply that I didn't at some level feel the sting of loneliness, an earthly longing to know another and be known; but at the same time, in those moments—and they were often—I quickly let His love remind me that I *was* known and that He could be whatever I needed if I would press into Him.

People wondered if I'd be open to a set-up or a blind date. You single gals know the drill; everyone has *someone* that "You've just got to meet!" I let someone get close but over the course of a few months, we knew it just wasn't what God had for each of us. All that was a little too much for my wounded heart, and I decided it was best for me to guard my heart like never before. Why even pursue love when I knew He was meant to satisfy? I didn't need another heartbreak. I didn't need another area to heal; I was still healing as it was. From then on, I put my blinders on, and I was full speed ahead.

RUTH

Then the Lord introduced me to a woman in the Bible that I could relate to—Ruth. Her story struck a chord with me. I never imagined living my life as a young widow, so finding one within the pages of God's love story, with an entire book illuminating her life, made me tune in. I wondered what was so unique about this young girl that made the Lord determined to teach us through her life. I found myself connecting with her, understanding her pain, and watching her movements and responses. Her dedication to Naomi was beautiful, and her confidence in spite of her upside-down world gave me strength to follow even when it didn't make sense.

I attended a conference where Jackie Kendall, speaker and author, spoke to young women about finding a real-life Boaz. In the book of Ruth, Boaz is a striking depiction of Christ with his compassion to provide, his love that protects, and his choice to redeem. Jackie lightheartedly cautioned us to avoid the Bozos and seek our own Boaz. Girls snatched up t-shirts and books to remind them to be on the lookout for their own Boaz.

I left there in awe that God had been my real-life Boaz. He was mine, and He protected me, provided for me, and in a most magnificent way, had redeemed me! Others said to me, "That's great, but don't you want to meet someone? Aren't you open to loving another?"

My response? A canned motto that I lived by: "This is what I want: I want what God wants. I had a great marriage to James. Even though we only got to experience one year of marriage together, it was amazing. So I consider myself blessed to have experienced that kind of love. If God calls me to be single, I would be great with that; if not, I'm sure I'd be great with that as well."

It was easier for my heart to just let Him handle the dreaming. If I could shut off any dreams and desires, I would never be disappointed again. Right? I honestly didn't want to miss anything He had for me but it was safer to live with no expectations.

Killing my desires may have started small, but I found it a much easier way to live. Without any real dreams of my own, there was no let down! Anytime I started to daydream, I quickly reprimanded myself and gave myself an internal pep talk to get my heart and mind realigned. This was tedious at first, but after a while it just came naturally. I found myself busy with life and thankful for His dreams for me. But was He really calling me to kill my heart and all its desires? Allow me to share with you how I came to meet an earthly Boaz.

MINDING MY
OWN BUSINESS

Many great people encouraged me on this journey, and some I fondly refer to as my cheerleaders. One near and dear to my heart is a woman by the name of Glenda. I find myself saying often, "Everyone needs a Glenda!" My move to Springfield was hard on me on all levels, but by God's grace and through her obedience, He used this woman as a mighty source of support.

She had worked with these teens for years, and as I was taking on some of those leadership roles, she swept into my life and pulled me under her wing. She was married with one son, yet she hadn't married until a bit later in life so she knew the loneliness a single young woman bore. The most beautiful friendship and mentorship developed as she spoke into my life in a way no one had done before her. She had been in youth ministry for years and was seasoned and knowledgeable, and she could sense I was in need of rest and companionship. Because she consistently gave to me, I was able to continually give to others. I affectionately call her my "other mother," and she gave me permission to be a mess with her, so I wouldn't be a mess in front of many. She often invited me to share dinner with her family with her added promise, "Then we'll talk until we've solved all the world's problems." She was my counselor in so many areas. We would talk about the teens we worked with, what God was teaching us, or what we were struggling with. Her listening ear and wise counsel kept me grounded and pressing into the Lord daily. She quickly earned the right to say whatever she pleased in my life, and I was thankful for her boldness with me, stemming from her zeal for the Lord.

Boys entered our conversations from time to time, and she told me often that she couldn't wait to see who God had for me. She would go as far as saying, "When it happens ..." and then smile and joke about my wedding day, how she would cry, and how it would feel as though she was watching her daughter getting married. She would dream out loud about how amazing he was going to have to be. I would smile and sometimes try to laugh her words off, but other times my guarded heart deeply wanted to beg her to stop because she stirred up emotion in me. Sometimes I would reply with my motto, "Whatever God wants. If I'm single? Great. If He has someone? Great." But when I tried to stop her, she would, in her confident and self-assured way, tell me that God was preparing someone for me and that she couldn't wait!

After a year and a half at the church, I really needed some more peer relationships. Time with sixteen-year-olds is great, but I was always the one giving, and God knew that to be able to give, I needed to have a balance of giving and receiving. I decided to be more intentional with getting to know others on a deeper level in my same stage of life, for it was unhealthy for me to surround myself solely with the teens. After hearing many pleadings and soapbox sermons from Glenda, I connected with the young adult ministry at church. I knew many already from my time there and was lovingly invited to gatherings and Sunday lunches.

I made friends with several young adults, and one in particular had been a friend since the first time I stepped foot in the church's building—a guy by the name of Dallas. He was a leader in the young adult ministry and had also helped many times with our annual Disciple Now weekends we'd held for the youth. Before I even moved to Springfield, my sisters and I had come down during one of those weekends to give a concert and share our testimonies, so over the last few years Dallas and I had crossed paths many times. Dallas stood out among his peers not only because he was extremely tall but also because of his reputation as a kind and approachable shepherd and leader. He was significant in getting me connected. I still had limited time because of my activities with the youth and a side job, but I tried to find time to devote to the young adult get-togethers a few times a month.

Lunch with girlfriends or a movie night with the young adults was always fun. On one of these lunches, I was asked, "What do you think about Dallas?"

"Wow, what a nice guy! He's great," I responded.

I choked a bit on my next bite as she said, "He'd really like to get to know you more. He said it would be okay if I let you know what he'd been thinking."

I was a bit in shock, because he was *Dallas*—a friend, a guy from church. I managed to say, "I'm honored, I guess. He is an amazing guy." She just sat there smiling until I said, "I don't know. I've never really thought about him in that way." My blinders and my guarded heart told me to be flattered and move on.

After an awkward encounter with Dallas a few days later, I agreed to hang out sometime, but I truly didn't want to. I've never liked confrontation or being the bearer of bad news, but I've always been transparent, so when I said yes, he could read the true response all over my face. Needless to say, we never hung out.

I dove into my busy schedule with the youth. I didn't have much time to commit to anything else, and strapping on my blinders a bit tighter and heading on my way felt the most comfortable. After a loaded summer of camps, mission trips, and chaperoning a senior-high trip, I found myself again running on empty and needing some time with others my own age.

Seven months after our awkward exchange, I resurfaced and was relieved to find things seemed to have been forgotten. I considered Dallas a good friend, and I was blessed to have other friends my age and to also love the ministry God had given me.

I longed to go on a mission trip outside the youth ministry where I could be part of a team rather than lead a team, and where I could experience another culture. An opportunity for church members to go mountain biking through the jungles of Costa Rica and deliver the gospel of John to homes along those dirt roads arose. This seemed a bit extreme for me, but I wanted to be obedient in the gifts God had blessed me with. Even though I had never mountain biked, I thought I could give of myself physically for the sake of spreading the gospel. I prayed about it, and though I was extremely nervous, I signed up. This was the church's first missionary adventure like this, so the group was kept small and manageable. Who knew that Dallas was also among those going?

As I peddled up mountains and down steep terrain, I saw God everywhere. When I approached houses and delivered the gospel of John to mountainside homes, I was more aware of God's demonstrative pursuit for all of us. How great He must love these people to send us—a couple of mid-Missourians to travel to another country, memorize some key sentences in Spanish, and ride bikes sometimes ten hours a day just to express this love. I was used to feeling alone in ministry, but on this trip I gained a companion.

Dallas looked out for me, for my well-being; he was truly a servant to not only me but to the entire team. He was experienced, but more than that, he watched out for those that were weak, and I was weak. Some days, while everyone was loading their bikes for the day, I found my bike completely taken care of. Mud from the previous day was washed away and my water bottles were filled. I felt protected and thought of during those intense days of sweat and tears. Our friendship continued to grow, but his way of caring for me made me feel vulnerable. At times I was drawn to this pursuit; other times I ran like a scared little rabbit.

On the way home, we sat on the plane together, and as we neared our destination, he said, "I'm sure you can tell that I am fond of you. You don't need to say a thing; I'm not looking for a response, but I felt like it is proper and right to at least let you know how I feel about you." I was speechless. I stumbled over a few words and ums and ohs, but I eventually ended by saying that I had enjoyed getting to know him more and that I noticed myself drawn to him as well. I couldn't believe I was saying that! But it was true, even if I was about to run again.

I hugged him goodbye that night and knew that I had let the intensity of the week get to me emotionally. We spent more time together talking on the phone and getting a bite to eat once in a while, but I had no intention of letting him have my heart. This wasn't fair to him, and I finally decided to let him know.

While I was on the phone with a friend, I told her, "I just need to tell him. The next time I see him, I'll tell him." We weren't even off the phone when I heard my doorbell. There he was! When I opened the door, he had flowers in hand. I was speechless. I stumbled through my thank you, but I knew he could see me struggling. I was getting ready to leave for work, and this wasn't the right time to get into a long conversation, so we parted ways. As I drove to work, I knew what I had to do. I called him and asked to see him after I got home that night. I wasn't being fair to him. He was wasting his affection on the wrong girl.

The moment of truth. If anyone ever had a right to use the line, "It's not you. It's me," it was me. I told him that I truly cared about him but that I didn't think my heart could care about him in the same way he cared for me. I tried my best to communicate my feelings, but I just couldn't. I was surprised by his reaction! Yes, he was surprised and disappointed, but I mostly heard frustration in his voice. He was confused because he really felt the Lord had led him to pursue me, and he was puzzled as to why I felt the way I did. He simply said, "You never even tried."

We discussed changes that would have to take place, and my heart grew sad. I didn't want to give up our friendship because it meant so much to me, but I felt I could only ever be a friend to him. We both felt the loss and the pain and began to cry; my guarded heart wasn't as untouchable as I had hoped. I looked at him through my tears, and I reached out and put my hand on his. Something in my heart broke. I saw *him* for the first time, and my heart filled with love. Yes, I loved him as a friend, but this was deeper.

Dallas told me something he had been carrying for a long time that he had never shared with me—something that happened even before our trip to Costa Rica. One Saturday morning he was praying about his feelings for me, and he asked the Lord to teach him how to pray for me. That morning he felt the Lord direct him to go to West Plains, Missouri. The Lord was leading him to the cemetery to find James's gravestone. After getting information at a visitor's center, he found the cemetery. He walked for a while, but because there was no one on duty, he was just left to wander; after walking around for an hour, he realized he couldn't find it on his own. He headed back to his car, asking the Lord to help him find it, and he saw it as he was walking past. He knelt down at James's headstone and prayed for me. Dallas told me that the Lord had led him to that place so he could better understand what I went through and what I had lost.

As he shared that with me, God did something in me that I will ever cherish. God taught me to love again. He showed me what it meant to be genuinely pursued and sought after. He tore down my walls and allowed me to experience redeeming love. Dallas had described me as Sleeping Beauty to his mother and told her that he believed he had been sent to wake me up. That night I awoke and saw my prince. God taught us both a great deal in those months leading up to that night. Did He allow my walls to remain high so Dallas could understand more about God's unrelenting pursuit and love for us? Did He want me to be awakened on that night, or had I missed the blessing that was there all along? I don't have all the answers, but I share my story of redeeming love to let you in on our testimony of God's grace.

From that moment on, the walls were down, and our hearts surrendered to God's will. Most of my friends' heads were spinning. The night before they heard me say I planned to tell Dallas I didn't think I could like him like that, and the next thing they heard was, "I think I'm crazy about him." Sometimes I couldn't believe the words that were coming out of my mouth, but I kept asking the Lord to give me wisdom and discernment as I moved forward in this relationship. We were married seven months later, celebrating God's story and our new role as husband and wife.

The Brills' role in our ceremony was one of the most beautiful parts of our wedding. Jim and Penny Brill are family, and they have been incredible mentors and parents to me. My father wasn't there to give me away this time, but I still wanted a father figure to walk with me arm-and-arm down the aisle. Jim was that person. I was nervous to ask him, and I wanted him to think and pray about it, but without hesitation, he said, "I don't have to think about it. I have prayed about this day. I'd love to!"

It meant so much to have them there supporting me, getting to know Dallas and sharing what God had done in our lives. The entire day was a celebration of redeeming love, a picture of Christ loving the church and pledging His life to her.

Dallas and I married in 2004. Did we *happen* to meet each other and fall in love?

> And (Ruth) happened to come to the portion of the field belonging to Boaz.
>
> *Ruth 2:3 (NASB)*

God has a story to tell, and He desires to use us to share Himself with the world. In a sermon, John Piper says,

"Ruth *happened* to come to Boaz's field because God is gracious and sovereign even when he is silent. As the proverb says, 'A man's mind plans his way, but the Lord directs his steps'" (16:9).

Know this: Even when you think you are the one making the decisions and moving forward, God is the one who directs our steps. He is full of grace even when we deserve none. He has a plan, and you are in it. Even when you try to abandon dreaming all together, His desire is to make your God-given, God-sized dreams come true. He wants great things for your life, and He is willing to write an amazing story from one that's already begun.

> For I am confident of this very thing, that He who began a good work in you will perfect it until the day of Christ Jesus.
>
> *Philippians 1:6 (NASB)*

HE SEES—
A MODERN-DAY HAGAR

Holly

When I stood at the front of a church in March of 1996, looking into the eyes of my husband, committing, "for better or worse, until death do us part," I never would have guessed that four years later I would find myself staring at a closed casket that contained the face of the one I loved so dearly. I found myself in a desert or wilderness of loneliness as a single mom, roaming aimlessly. At times I even felt exiled from previous friends and family. So many people didn't know how to reach out to Heather and I.

"Does God see me? Does He care?" my heart would cry. Truthfully, I always knew the answers to these questions. I was just so desperate to hear that He had not forgotten me. I needed to hear again that He had special plans for my life and for the sweet life Scott left behind in Emma. What was going to happen to her? Could I raise her alone?

I believe many times we remember God's promises to us in our lives or the things we've believed He has revealed to us as our specific "calling" or purpose, but our current circumstances don't seem to match up or seem on a completely different highway with where we're supposed to be headed. Sometimes we have to go through hurdles and obstacles for God to release a new phase in our life. He's building us up for who He needs us to become and what He needs us to do. I believe that when God allows us to go through the greatest pain and trials in our lives, He's simply preparing us to achieve the greatest triumph and victory. We just need to hold on and be patient as He works things out. God watches over His Word to perform it. We can believe His promises, and His words are true.

Recently, Aaron and I have been studying the names of God for a series we've been teaching at our church. Since the beginning of our study, we are becoming so much more aware of who God is and what He does. I've seen my faith rise in my personal prayer life as I understand what once were mysteries to me now have become so much clearer. The word "Elohim," for instance, is the name for God as our Creator. The God who speaks and it happens. It's used over 2,500 times in the Bible. "Yahweh" or "Jehovah" is the covenant name for God. Scholars have learned that this name was once considered so sacred and so holy that men wouldn't dare pronounce it. This name of God is recorded more than 6,800 times in Scripture. We often sing songs that depict who God is in "Jehovah Jireh," our Provider, or "Jehovah Rapha," our Healer; but one of the names that stands out to me the most in my study is "El Roi," the God who sees. This name is only used one time in Scripture. It's almost like a hidden treasure or precious nugget in the Bible.

In Genesis chapter 16, you'll find the story of a slave girl named Hagar. In most instances, she's not the focal point of the story, but her life has really stood out and spoken to me. She was a single mom who found herself alone in the desert in a situation that was totally not of her choosing. When I think of a desert, I think of a land that is barren and dry. A desert is a place that has no life. At this time in my life, I have no doubt that I have shared a lot of the same feelings that Hagar felt. I felt as though I had no life! Nothing inside of me felt like it was bearing fruit. I found myself in a situation that I did not choose, just like Hagar.

You probably remember the story. God had promised Abram and Sarai that they would have a son from whom many nations would come, but Abram and Sarai became a little impatient. So Sarai encouraged Abram to sleep with her maid, Hagar, to get her pregnant so they could begin their family that God promised. The problem is, they didn't trust God and His timing. They took matters into their own hands.

Oswald Chambers says in his book *My Utmost for His Highest*[10], "Whenever God gives a vision to a saint, He puts him, as it were, in the shadow of His hand, and the saint's duty is to be still and listen. There is darkness which comes from excess of light, and then is the time to listen. Genesis 16 is an illustration of listening to good advice when it is dark instead of waiting for God to send the light. When God gives a vision and darkness follows, *wait.* God will make you in accordance with the vision He has given if you will wait for His time. Never try and help God fulfill His word." *A delay is not necessarily a denial!*

Hagar does indeed become pregnant, and tension rises between her and Sarai. Sarai, in return for Hagar's blatant disrespect, becomes extremely mean to Hagar. Who knows? Maybe Hagar wanted nothing to do with all of this in the first place. And at this point, she was carrying a child, feeling alone, and decided to leave.

What is your situation even now as you read this book? Do you feel alone, rejected? Do you wonder if anyone cares for you or *sees* you? Do you feel like you're walking in a wilderness with no way out? Be encouraged by Hagar's story!

> An angel of God found her beside a spring in the desert; it was the spring on the road to Shur. He said, "Hagar, maid of Sarai, what are you doing here?"
>
> She said, "I'm running away from Sarai, my mistress."

The angel of God said, "Go back to your mistress. Put up with her abuse." He continued, "I'm going to give you a big family, children past counting. From this pregnancy, you'll get a son: Name him Ishmael; for God heard you, God answered you....

She answered God by name, praying to the God who spoke to her, "You're the God (El Roi) who sees me! Yes! He saw me; and then I saw Him!"

Genesis 16:7–13 *(MSG)*

So here we see in the previous verses that the angel of God (we know by reading this story more is that this is God, the pre-incarnate Christ) *found* her. I think it's interesting that the scripture uses the word "found," because we obviously know that God is omniscient and omnipresent. God is always aware where we are and what we're going through. The Hebrew word for found refers to "finding someone or something that is lost or misplaced." Certainly Hagar must have felt both lost and misplaced. She was alone in a barren desert wilderness, pregnant with a child because of another person's willful desire; but she was not alone, because the angel of the Lord found her. This is where God so often finds us. We're in crazy situations, tangled in a web of hopelessness and despair, and it's as if you can hear God say to you, *What are you doing here? What's going on in your life?*

God tells Hagar to return and submit. We can run to God and complain and cry out to Him, throwing our arms up in the air admitting surrender, and He listens to us. And then when we're finished with our tantrum, God's response may be, *Child, I hear you, but I need to first help you fix some areas in your life before I fix your situation.*

In April of 2008 I became very sick. At first I thought it just might be food poisoning or the flu, but over a series of a few days, I could tell I needed to get to a doctor. Aaron was on his way to a Dallas Mavericks game that night with a friend. Before he left, I convinced him and myself that I would be fine—I knew he was in real need of some down time. As he was on his way, I called him and asked him to come back home and take me to the doctor.

Aaron took me to a Care Now clinic after we found friends from church to care for our children. After seeing a doctor, they called a local hospital and sent us on our way for immediate evaluation. They began many tests and decided to admit me overnight. In the following days, my symptoms violently increased, and they were considering giving me a blood transfusion due to a constant loss of blood. I remember thinking, *This can't be happening! How did I get here?*

The doctors were able to get me well enough to run some more tests and were able to determine that I had a serious disease for which there was not a cure, but it was treatable. The doctor began to tell Aaron and I what the rest of our lives would look like in caring for this disease. Fear and anxiety rose within me, but I'll never forget when Aaron brought me a DVD message from a pastor in the Dallas/Fort Worth area that had really ministered to him the night before. The message was about going through storms in your life. This pastor made a comment in his message that stopped me in my tracks. I knew this was for me. He said, "Sometimes God allows you to go through storms in your life to reveal your weaknesses." I broke. I sobbed and cried. I had always told Aaron in times past that it's easy to pray for other people. It's praying for myself that I struggled with. I almost wore that statement like a badge in the past. As if I was almost proud of that fact. How wrong I was! I felt God whisper to my spirit, *Holly, it's time to strengthen this area in your life. You will now pray for yourself like you've never prayed before and worship like you've never worshiped Me before through your actions.*

And that's exactly what I began to do. Not only that, I think I had one of my absolute favorite nights with Aaron that night in the hospital room. We prayed and cried together. I had never felt closer to anyone in my life. We sought God for my health and for our family and for our future. I began praying for my nurses and others in the hospital that I knew were hurting or sick. Aaron and I even felt God challenge us to worship Him in a new way. We began passing out many of our flower arrangements I had received while in the hospital to others in rooms near mine who were hurting and needed to be shown love. In one instance, I had just received flowers from Heather. They were some of my favorites, and Aaron and I saw a family who looked like they needed a little encouragement down the hall. I wasn't feeling well enough at that time to get up and take them with Aaron, but he really felt he was supposed to talk to them. He went over to them and said, "I just want to give these flowers to you."

The mother said, "Why would you do this?"

He responded, "I just felt like I was supposed to talk with you and encourage you."

She hung her head and began to tell Aaron that her husband had just passed away moments before he came to talk to them. He began to share with them about Jesus. How He loved them and had wonderful plans for their lives, and that He could see them right now and longed for them to reach out to Him. Aaron prayed with them. The mother of the family said that she would never forget what he had done that day.

Over the next few days, my strength grew, and Aaron's faith continued to rise. I was finally going to get to go home. I was signing my discharge papers and realized that the medication that I was supposed to be on for the rest of my life was not included. I asked the nurses about it, and they couldn't figure out why it wasn't with my paperwork. They called my doctor, and he informed them that he needed to talk to me before they let me leave. So Aaron and I waited.

The doctor made it to my room and began to shake his head. He said, "Holly, I don't understand it. I saw what I saw. I've been in this field for years. But the lab is telling me that there is nothing wrong with you. So based on what they're telling me, I can't give you this medicine, but I want to re-check you in a few weeks."

He walked out of the room. Aaron and I looked at each other and began to cry. I wanted to scream and shout! We both knew that God had healed my sick body. El Roi saw me and heard my cries.

God saw Hagar that day in the wilderness just like He saw me in that hospital bed. He saw her hurt and despair. He promised her a son that He would bless. It's easy to feel like Hagar—like nobody cares or sees what you're going through; but there is a God named El Roi who sees you. He cares about everything that you're going through.

Although we only see this name one time in Scripture, we see this principle all throughout the Bible. For example, Matthew 10:29–31:

> Are not two sparrows sold for a penny? And not one of them will fall to the ground apart from the Father. But even the hairs of your head are numbered. Fear not, therefore, you are of more value than many sparrows.

In biblical times the sparrow was considered a cheap little bird. Luke's gospel says that if you bought four, then you would get a fifth one for free. The word "fall" could also mean hop, in this passage. He sees when they hop and when they stop hopping. Nothing escapes God's notice! The average person has 140,000 hairs on their head. God cares about every little detail of your life. Psalm 139 says it so well,

> O Lord, you have examined my heart and know everything about me.
>
> You know when I sit down or stand up. You know my every thought when far away.
>
> You chart the path ahead for me and tell me where to stop and rest. Every moment you know where I am.
>
> You know what I am going to say even before I say it, Lord.

You both precede and follow me. You place your hand of blessing on my head.

Such knowledge is too wonderful for me, too great for me to know!

I can never escape from your spirit! I can never get away from your presence!

If I go up to heaven, you are there; if I go down to the place of the dead, you are there.

If I ride the wings of the morning, if I dwell by the farthest oceans, even there your hand will guide me, and your strength will support me.

I could ask the darkness to hide me and the light around me to become night–But even in darkness I cannot hide from you.

To you the night shines as bright as day. Darkness and light are both alike to you.

You made all the delicate, inner parts of my body and knit me together in my mother's womb.

Thank you for making me so wonderfully complex! Your workmanship is marvelous–and how well I know it.

You watched me as I was being formed in utter seclusion, as I was woven together in the dark of the womb.

You saw me before I was born. Every day of my life was recorded in your book.

Every moment was laid out before a single day had passed.

How precious are your thoughts about me, O God! They are innumerable!

I can't even count them; They outnumber the grains of sand!

And when I wake up in the morning, you are still with me!

There's no doubt that God knew exactly how Hagar was feeling. His eye was always watching over her. After she returned to Abram and Sarai, she discovered that God fulfilled His promise to them, and they became pregnant with Isaac. Sarai (who is now renamed Sarah) wants Hagar and Ishmael out of there! So Abraham does what his wife wishes and sends them off. Once again Hagar finds herself in the desert with her son, Ishmael; only now, she fears that they won't make it.

> Abraham got up early the next morning, got some food together and a canteen of water for Hagar, put them on her back and sent her away with the child. She wandered off into the desert of Beersheba. When the water was gone, she left the child under a shrub and went off, fifty yards or so. She said, "I can't watch my son die." As she sat, she broke into sobs.
>
> Meanwhile, God heard the boy crying. The angel of God called from heaven to Hagar, "What's wrong, Hagar? Don't be afraid. God has heard the boy and knows the fix he's in. Up now; go get the boy. Hold him tight. I'm going to make of him a great nation."
>
> Just then God opened her eyes. She looked. She saw a well of water. She went to it and filled her canteen and gave the boy a long, cool drink.
>
> God was on the boy's side as he grew up. He lived out in the desert and became a skilled archer.
>
> *Genesis 21:14–20 (MSG)*

The God who sees opened her eyes! What was once unclear, He makes clear. What seems impossible, He makes possible! This is what is awesome about prayer.

You can be praying about something where there seems to be no way of working it out, no answer; then suddenly God brings clarity to the situation. The God who sees, opens your eyes. You find the answer you've been looking for, staring you down so plainly. The way that text reads, it makes you think that the well of water had been there the whole time, but God opened her eyes and that's when she saw it. Don't you think that is often the case in our lives? The answer may be right in front of us, but until God opens our eyes, we just can't see it.

Satan wants to make you think that God doesn't see you or care about your situations. He is the one who makes you feel alone in a desert and full of despair. But be encouraged. El Roi sees you even now, and He cares about you. The answer that you think is so unreachable, or the situation that seems like it will never correct itself, may be just before you. Ask God to open your eyes and make things clear.

R.C. Sproul says, "There are many things in my life that I do not want to put under the gaze of Christ. Yet I know there is nothing hidden from Him. He knows me better than my wife knows me. And yet He loves me. This is the most amazing thing of all about God's grace. It would be one thing for Him to love us if we could fool Him into thinking that we were better than we actually are. But He knows better. He knows all there is to know about us, including those things that could destroy our reputation. He is minutely and acutely aware of every skeleton in every closet. And He loves us."[11]

I don't know your situation. Answers that you may

have to life's questions may never make themselves clear. But I know God sees. But it's not just that He sees. We serve a God who is compassionate and desperate to show His love to His children. Recently, we received word that a man in our church was murdered at his business one night as he was closing up. He was brutally attacked, robbed, then murdered. He is survived by a wife and five children. I can't imagine sorting through that emotionally, physically, and spiritually. I even find myself saying to myself when I hear that someone has lost a spouse, "Wow! I can't imagine that." Then I register the reality of what has happened in my life and what's just come out of my mouth and realize that *I have* been through that. But the fact is, God has done an amazing job healing those wounds and that hurt. Is it completely gone? No. Do I still miss Scott? Absolutely. However, sometimes that part of my life just seems like a bad dream. I don't say that to seem shallow or hurtful, but to me, it gives even more glory to my beautiful God! He's the one who has done this work in my life. He has restored my life. He has brought me new purpose!

Can you imagine what it was like for Hagar to hear God call out to her again? God wanted to reveal to her that first He did in fact hear her and her son, and He was going to do something about it. He didn't just supply water to sustain them; He promised Hagar that her son would make a great nation. God had a plan. He opened her eyes and then exceeded her wildest expectations for her son by making a nation from him.

God sees you today. He wants to bless you beyond

anything you could think or imagine. Maybe you are a single parent stretching every dollar to make this month's rent. Maybe you have lost a son or daughter, and their loss has left a giant hole in your heart. Perhaps you've recently gone through a divorce and feel like a train wreck. None of these situations are beyond God's repair. Just as His eye was on Hagar, His eye is watching over you. Cry out to Him today. Let Him hear your voice. Watch Him respond and care for your needs. Your answer may be right in front of you. Ask Him to open your eyes. He can be the "lifter" of your head.

> But You, O Lord, are a shield about me, my glory, and the lifter of my head.
>
> *Psalm 3:3 (TAB)*

DREAM A LITTLE DREAM FOR ME

My days have passed, my plans are shattered, and so
are the desires of my heart.

Job 17:11 (NIV)

Faith looks back and draws courage; hope looks
ahead and keeps desires alive.

John Eldridge[12]

Today if you hear His voice, do not harden your
hearts ... So we see that they were not able to enter
because of unbelief.

Hebrews 3:15,19 (NAS)

Heather

The other night I had a dream that Satan went to our church. I know, I know. Honestly, what did I eat before bed? But seriously, he was loud and obnoxious, and people knew who he was. He would annoy and disturb everyone around him in the service. He had already invaded our small groups, ruined relationships, destroyed marriages, and acted friendly to draw in others so he could whisper lies in their ears.

We finally met one day, but he didn't look at all like I pictured him—no horns or pitchfork. You know those loud, obnoxious guys who are always looking for an argument? That's who he reminded me of. He had a pride about him. In a boisterous tone, he started asking me questions about my faith, and to my surprise, he even said some things that I agreed with. In retrospect, I see that was only his game; he wanted me to think we believed the same so he could draw me in, and so I would begin questioning all God had said about him. Fortunately the Lord gave me discernment, and I was able to see through his patronizing lies.

Satan got so mad that I wasn't crumbling to his efforts that finally the mask came off, and I saw his scary side. This is usually the time—typically while I'm witnessing something frightening on television—that I cover my eyes, only leaving a crack between two fingers to see a little of what is happening. Usually I cower in fear, but this time I stood up, and I was surprisingly calm and collected. He swelled with power and seemed to enlarge to three times his size, but there I stood, almost with a smile on my face. Not afraid, not taken aback, strong. In my heart I knew God was with me and in me, so I need not fear. Satan began taunting me, seeing what would get to me, and he reminded me that he had literally taken lives before and that he'd do it again, right there, right then. But I stood with a peace inside me that God was my invincible army; no one, not even Satan, could get to me without God having a say in it. And honestly, if God chose to allow Satan to kill me, I was okay with that. He could take my life, but he couldn't take my soul. It already belonged to someone else.

I awoke and said to myself, "Well, that was weird." Obviously, I'm a vivid dreamer. Dallas gets a kick out of asking me each morning where I've been or what I've been up to. Some of my dreams are probably the result of poor eating right before bed, but others are more than that. I prayed a prayer a while ago, simply asking God to use even the hours that I sleep to show me more about who He is. I didn't want to waste a moment of Him. Maybe that's what I get: Satan coming to church.

I've always had vivid dreams at night regardless of life's circumstances. Something happened, however, that stole my freedom to dream about what God might have for my life. I became uncomfortable with nourishing the wishes, hopes, and desires in my heart.

DREAMING

I was now a wife again! My life had totally flipped upside down with this new love for Dallas. Had I expected it? No. Did I feel grateful and blessed? Very much so. But on our honeymoon, the Lord spoke something very powerful over my life. I was sitting on the beach in Playa del Carmen, listening to the waves crashing on the shore, gazing all around at God's beautiful creation. I had spent some time that morning reading, but I closed the book to talk to Him. It was hot in the sun, and Dallas leaned over and wiped my brow with a towel and pulled me in and gave me a little kiss. I leaned back in my chair and wondered to the Lord what I did to deserve this. I quickly sensed a response to my wonderings, "There was nothing you did to deserve this."

I quickly agreed, "You're absolutely right, Lord! Thank You, God, for this amazing husband. What a gift from you!"

He said, "You didn't dream of him."

"No, Lord, I didn't."

Without hesitation, the Lord responded, "I need you to start dreaming now."

I was silenced, and in an instant I understood that the Lord wasn't referring to the next time I fell asleep. He was talking about so much more. I knew in my heart what He was saying to me, but I was somewhat shocked at this command. I always thought I had been honoring the Lord by just letting Him be in charge of my life's dreams and desires, but I was not letting Him have control of this area like I initially thought; instead, because of the fear of yet another heartbreak, I found it easier to kill the very gift that He had given me—the gift of dreaming.

God didn't intend for us to live in defense mode, shutting off all feelings that lead to dreaming and fulfilling desires. Killing our hearts little by little was not what He meant by guarding our hearts (Proverbs 4:23). God Himself is a dreamer. He has dreams for our lives. Jeremiah 29:11 speaks beautifully of these dreams, plans, and hopes for us. God hadn't asked me to kill my life dreams; He just wanted to be in charge of fulfilling them in His timing, by His design. It was easier to believe that if I didn't hope or dream of things to come, I wouldn't be let down. But like I've admitted, instead of allowing myself to learn through heartache, I tried my hardest to rid opportunity of disappointment by not pursuing the hopes that would arise in my heart; and as a defense mechanism, I stopped dreaming. Let me explain.

It's very normal for a woman in her twenties to hope to grow old with a husband. But I didn't. It's normal to hope to be a mother. But I didn't. I felt embarrassed and even pain if I let my heart go there. I was scared to move, fearful of stepping out of turn, fearful of being disappointed yet again. I took the old saying to heart, "Don't get your hopes up!" And although there's some truth to that, I took it to a dangerous level, allowing sin and the evil one to distort what it looks like to have healthy, God-honoring hope alive in my heart. I reasoned that without hope, without daydreaming of things to come, I was humbling myself before Him. To humble oneself before the will of the Lord looks and feels different than complete abdication of all dreams and desires.

He hadn't created me to be a puppet on a string; He wanted me to have an active part in attempting great things for Him. *Dream, child!* But at some level I had forgotten how. I had let that part of my heart become so dead that I didn't know how to start. I now can see that if you feel guilty hoping, there's obviously some healing that needs to occur.

> He tears me down on every side till I am gone; he uproots my hope like a tree.
>
> *Job 19:10 (NIV)*

A COUPLE QUESTIONS

So how do we begin to hope when we are still living in the shadow of shattered dreams? What if we were dreamers once before but are now too afraid to let our hearts wander to those places for fear of another disappointment and yet another heartbreak?

For me, God presented me with a challenge. He wanted this dreamer to dream, but the journey required answering a few of His questions. The first, "Do you trust *Me?*" That question seemed easy to answer, "Lord, of course *You* can be trusted!" But that wasn't the question. He wanted to know if *I* could trust Him personally. Indeed, my heart had been wounded, my dreams completely dashed, and my plans gone in an instant, but even as I embraced some of the change that had been forced upon me, there were times not long after losing James that I quickly began dreaming new dreams.

I tried to imagine what I could do for Him or what He was going to ask of me. At some level I was terrified, reminded of my still-healing heart. A few times I tested the water. I would move forward, pursuing a dream or walking through an open door only to encounter yet another abrupt halt. Doors that stood wide open for a moment would close without warning, causing me to rethink pursuing my dreams all together. I instead chose to learn how to *not* dream for the sole purpose of guarding my heart from disappointment.

But there on the beach, God was calling me to face my fears: no sure things, no earthly absolutes, and no formulas—just cold, hard trust. "Do you trust that I have good things in store for you? Do you trust that I have a plan that is better than your plan? Do you believe I am who I say I am? Are you going to live believing Me or live doubting Me?"

Stepping over this hurdle sounds easy, but there are roadblocks. How do you answer some of these questions? Are you scared to trust Him for fear of what He's going to call you to? Are you a control freak? Does it frighten you at the mere thought of not being the one to call the shots? Or have you wondered if He is worthy of your trust? I've been there. I've wrestled with these questions. I've come to these roadblocks, and honestly, I'm ashamed to admit, I let some of them keep me from moving forward. I've consulted my wounded heart more often than I care to admit. I've stayed put many times for fear of what may lie ahead. But the truth will make itself known, and we won't be able to hide from Him or His Word for long. And it's what we do with that truth that will illuminate our true response to His questions.

> May the God of hope fill you with all joy and peace as you trust in him, so that you may overflow with hope by the power of the Holy Spirit.
>
> *Romans 15:13 (NIV)*

> If your law had not been my delight, I would have perished in my affliction.
>
> *Psalm 119:92 (NIV)*

He gave us His Word, this love letter, for a reason. And it was through searching Him out that I found my answer. I'm thankful that He is consistent throughout Scripture, desperate to communicate His love to His people, delighting in displaying this love, and confident that He has a purpose and plan for our lives.

> This is God's Word on the subject: "I know what I'm doing. I have it all planned out—plans to take care of you, not abandon you, plans to give you the future that you hope for."
>
> *Jeremiah 29:10–11 (MSG)*

By opening His Word every day, I found peace in trusting Him. When things don't seem to be going right or falling into line, it's tempting to lose heart along the way, to throw in the towel and commit to finding your own way through this life. But if you are *in* His Word, He is always there reminding you that there will be times when it is easier to doubt or stumble, but His promise remains: If you don't lose heart, you will reap a harvest of blessing at the appropriate time (Galations 6:9).

When you engross yourself with His Word and let your heart engage its truth, even if it is to find out if He's trustworthy, you end up finding reassurance that He is who He says He is, and that He is about good and perfect things. Trusting someone like that ends up being quite easy, even when things look blurry at times or simply make no sense. He says He is always faithful, for He cannot disown Himself (2 Timothy 2:13). By His very nature He is faithful, and if He were anything less, that would make Him ungodly—denying Himself. We may turn our backs on Him, but it's not in Him to do the same to us. Whether or not we choose to trust him, He will always be worthy of our trust; that will never change. His Word and His actions speak loud and clear.

Which leads me to His second question. If He has proved beyond a shadow of a doubt that He *can* be trusted, the next fair question is, "Can *you* be trusted?" He was asking me if I was going to be faithful with the small things, with the hard things, with the very dreams and hopes He had placed in my heart. He may be asking you the same question. Are you going to live a life that says that you trust Him, that you follow Him, and that you will testify with your lips and with your life that He is all that He claims to be?

If you falter in times of trouble, how small is your strength!

Proverbs 24:10 (NIV)

Do you remember the passage in Matthew where a master went on a journey and before leaving called his servants together to divvy up some talents? To one he gave five talents; to another, two; to another, one; he gave to "each according to his own abilities; and immediately he went on a journey" (Matthew 25:14–15). Do you remember what happened? By the time the master returned, the first one went out and doubled his five talents. The second, same story; his return was double what he was given. The last servant, when the master returned, offered this response: "Master, I knew that you are a hard man, harvesting where you have not sown and gathering where you have not scattered seed. So I was afraid and went out and hid your talent in the ground. See, here is what belongs to you." And the master's response? He called him wicked and lazy.

I wonder how we view God. Do we have a healthy understanding of our standing with Him, or do we live in such fear of Him that we respond as this last servant? His question to me, "Can *you* be trusted," was the very question I believe the master in this story was asking his servants as he bestowed to them talents. The first two gave their response; they went out and showed that they could be trusted. They served their master and did not take their responsibility lightly. They were able to come back to him and offer a great return, pleasing their master. And his response, "Well done, good and faithful servant! You have been faithful with a few things; I will put you in charge of many things. Come and share your master's happiness." Wow. What a privilege to be among those who hear, "Well done, good and faithful servant!" I've pictured that day quite often, desiring to hear those words when I'm face-to-face with Christ. I know I haven't been perfect—far from it—but my heart's deepest desire is to please my Master. I don't want to miss it. I don't want to be holding on to a talent for fear I'll use it wrong and be punished for it. I want to be mindful of Who it is that bestowed this honor to me and Whom it is I'm working for. In Max Lucado's book, *Cure for the Common Life,* he says, "The one-talent servant never knew his master. He should have. He lived under his roof and shared his address. He knew his face, his name, but he never knew his master's heart. And, as a result, he broke it."[13]

How do you view God? That really is His first question, and it determines the answer to His second. How you view Him will determine how you respond to Him and how you live for Him. He has called us to dream not so He can trample those dreams to teach us lesson after lesson but to dream so we can live lives outside of our own strength and power, so we can see His glory revealed, and so we are forced to abide in His mind and in His Word, as it sets the groundwork for this great journey called the kingdom of God. He calls us to have vision, for "where there is no vision the people perish" (Proverbs 29:18 TAB). He didn't want me to live dead. He wanted me to find vision, purpose, and hope in the future that He had marked out for me.

I like playing it safe. I enjoy watching someone else do it first, so I can learn from them, but clearly that's not how faith works, I'm afraid. "Faith is the confidence that what we hope for will actually happen; it gives us assurance about things we cannot see" (Hebrews 11:1). Trust. Putting all your eggs in one basket. Confident even when we can't see a step ahead of us. This is not a road that leads to everything being easy, feeling right, or turning out the way you want them to. A journey down this road may be windy, may cause your heart to pound, and may be uphill much of the way, but in the end, it leads to a life beyond our wildest imaginations. Why? Because His ways are higher than ours, and His thoughts are beyond ours. He was giving me the choice to live out *His* wildest imaginations, believing that this faith that I said I had in Him would play out in my life, and that I could be a part of experiencing God-sized, God-centered, God-given dreams freely and frequently. When He's teaching us a lesson, believe that He usually puts it to the test.

MY TEST

Not long after Dallas and I were married, there were a handful of times as I would be spending time with the Lord, I kept feeling like He was saying to my spirit, *Heather, this dreaming requires you to step out in faith.* Honestly, I was confused. I thought, "What is He trying to tell me?" I felt as if I understood His desire for me to dream. At that point, I had surrendered to His call for me to begin dreaming, and I didn't feel like I was saying no to Him on anything. So what was this step of faith?

At the same time, I was reading *Dreams of a Woman*

by Sharon Jaynes, a book my friend Jewels gave me for Christmas. She said she hadn't really heard anything about it but that the Lord had led her to buy it for me. As I read it, this same call to step out in faith rose up within me, but when I asked God to clarify, it seemed that all I received in response was silence. I wondered if it had to do with dreaming but couldn't put my finger on it. On our honeymoon, I had told Dallas what I sensed God saying to me, and months later out of the blue he asked me, "So what have you been dreaming about?" At first I thought he was referring to my nightly adventures while I slept, but after he asked me again, I knew where he was headed.

"Um, I don't know. I think He's asking me to do something, but I'm not sure what it is." I told Dallas that I was trying to figure it out, and that I was actively pursuing hearing from Him and asking Him to teach me to dream outside of what was comfortable for me. Dallas's smile showed me that he had been praying very similar things for me.

A few days after that conversation, I went to lunch with my friend Amy; while we sat in the middle of Qdoba, she asked, "What's God been saying to you lately?" What a question! I love when friends want to dive in! I told her that I sensed without a doubt that He was calling me to step out in faith, but that He wasn't telling me exactly what to do.

"Are you sure?"

"Yeah, I'm stumped. I can't think of a single thing."

But she wouldn't quit. "You don't have any idea?

There's not something that He's put in your heart to do that would cause you to step out in faith?"

My mind quickly went to this one thing. *It couldn't be that, could it?* I stammered a bit and ended up saying, "Well, I guess there's this one thing, but I don't know." I couldn't believe I was saying it out loud! I had never shared these inner thoughts. Meekly, I suggested that God was asking me to write. There it was—out there. It was a dream He was awakening in me, but I hadn't even admitted it to myself for fear that I'd actually have to do it. I knew nothing about writing and nothing about where to start. Even Holly had brought up writing a week before my wedding, saying that she sensed that we were going to write our story together. I had laughed it off then, but Amy didn't laugh. She said, "I think you know what you're supposed to do." The Holy Spirit had put His finger on my shy and careful heart. Scared? That would be an understatement.

When I went home that night, my mind was going in a million different directions. *Could this be? How could I?* I suddenly felt like I had embarked on a very unstable tightrope and the enemy pounced on the opportunity. "That's silly. You can't do that. He can't be asking you to do something you're not even excited about. Maybe you are hearing Him wrong. You've made that mistake before! And remember all those doors you watched Him close time after time."

When Dallas got home from work, he started cooking dinner, while I sat at our kitchen table and filled him in on things of the day. I debated about telling him the details of my conversation with Amy, but I knew I had to.

"I think I figured out what God is trying to tell me. I mean, what He's calling me to do."

"Really? What is it?" he answered with a smile. At this moment, I decided to test God. Was that right? No, probably not. Was I acting on faith? Not really. But I'm thankful that God allows me to be silly at times and still covers my silliness with His amazing grace.

"You tell me what you think it is," I responded. If the Lord really wanted me to do this, I needed to know; I reasoned that Dallas and the Lord were pretty tight, so if God wanted me to move forward, He would reveal this to my husband as well.

Dallas looked over at me and said, "He wants you to write."

I burst into tears, dropped my head to the table, and cried, "Yeeeesss!"

I didn't start right away. I didn't know how. But I knew how to pray. I thanked the Lord for placing this dream in my heart, for being faithful even when I wasn't, and for calling me to accomplish something bigger than myself. I prayed about how, about when, and about what. Something about this dream to follow Him outside my comfort zone and into unknown territory felt good. Even though I hadn't started, just thinking about how He was going to accomplish this in me was freeing. I let myself daydream about how it might make Him smile when I was doing all that He had planned for me to do.

Two months later, the Lord woke me up in the middle of the night and gave me the words. My wrecked kingdom, an invitation to enter this King's kingdom, and a promise to bring me from death to life were perfectly articulated for me. I couldn't sleep, and for over an hour I thought back over my life, the lessons the Lord had taught me in the last five years, and how I'd truly seen Him. With my very eyes I had witnessed God. Among the ashes, through the storm, in His gentle whispers, and sometimes in the silence, I saw Him—I saw the Lord. The flood of words that overcame my soul had to be written down and given away. It was early—three o'clock in the morning—and I prayed, "Lord, help me remember this!" He responded, "Oh, no, Heather, get up."

> The Lord will work out his plans for my life—for your faithful love, O Lord, endures forever. Don't abandon me, for you made me.
>
> *Psalms 138:8 (NLT)*

Ever since my first early-morning wake-up call, my life has been filled with dreaming, and this book is a reflection of my dreams becoming reality. As I continue learning how dreaming looks and feels, God has awakened my heart to the mystery of who He is and the freedom of truly living in His plan. As I followed His lead and daydreamed on God's behalf, I watched Him do amazing things, things that are only possible through His Spirit.

In this fantastic adventure I'm embarking on, I am blown away at the things He is doing in, to, and through me. There have been many times the Lord has stopped me dead in my tracks and asked me to take in

His glory as He says, "Heather, this is what it looks like when you say yes to Me."

> They will be called oaks of righteousness, a planting
> of the Lord for the display of His splendor.
>
> *Isaiah 61:3 (NIV)*

If you are fearful, dive into God's Word and let His promises wash over your anxious heart. Allow Him to resurrect your wounded spirit to give you peace and joy as you begin dreaming again! God gives life—abundant life—overflowing! Job called Him the God who gives and takes away, but sometimes we focus on the taking away and forget that He is a loving God that gives!

The apostle John said, "There is no fear in love. But perfect love drives out fear, because fear has to do with punishment" (4:18). God doesn't plan to leave you bound to your disappointments; He plans to free you. So be ready to do all He has planned for you. If Satan rears his ugly head, and he will, remember my silly dream and stand firm—not afraid, not taken aback, strong and confident that God can and will give you the peace to combat his lies and to actively live out the dreams He has for you.

> "Without the anticipation of better things ahead,
> we will have no heart for the journey." [14]
>
> John Eldridge, *The Sacred Romance*

FROM WOUNDED TO DANCING

"He has sent me to bind up the brokenhearted."

–Jesus, Isaiah 61:1 (NIV)

A friend of mine who had also experienced tragedy asked me, "So when did you know that you were ready to dance?" I knew what she was asking; she wanted to know when her heart would stop aching and when her mind would stop playing out how life might have been if tragedy hadn't struck. I responded, "Dancing begins with a choice. It's not about being ready—you just have to choose to begin."

This dance for me began while I was still agonizing over gut-wrenching life issues, not after, and began as a desire welling up inside of me that can only be described as a need to worship not in spite of my pain but *through* my pain. The dancing, whether physical or spiritual, is an outward expression that occurs out of a heart desperate to articulate to God that it will choose to love Him even when it is broken or when the pain is too much to bear. It is a choice to live, move, and breath even when you don't think you have the strength. I told her, "I wish that I could tell you that at some point your heart will magically be unscathed and untouched, but the truth is, the healing occurs *through* the pain and in the dance." The more I learn about God, the more I begin to understand why we are wounded. We are wounded so that we can know Him intimately.

BIND UP

When Jesus said, "I have come to bind up the brokenhearted," what did He mean? The Hebrew word for "bind up" is *chavash,* meaning "to bind on, wrap around; bind up as a wound, bandage, cover, envelop, enclose." If I close my eyes, I can picture Jesus taking our wounds, bandaging them, and "binding up the brokenhearted." I could envision Him taking my aching, hemorrhaging heart and enclosing it within His hands, applying pressure on my wounded and bleeding heart until the flow of blood stopped. Now picture this, the very hands that compress our wounds are the nail-scarred hands of Christ! Does that not stop you in your tracks? Don't read any further until you've pictured the intimate implication here. He wants us to know and understand that He is personally aware of the pain we are feeling because He Himself was wounded.

He understands what a broken and devastated heart feels like because He carried our sin on His shoulders while those He came to save drove nails in His hands and feet, cursed and insulted Him, and called Him a liar. He bled love for us. Yet Jesus is the very One we raise our fist to and accuse of not caring!

The world offers advice on how to deal with a wounded heart: build up your walls, push everyone out, and don't let God near because you can't trust anyone but yourself! That's not what He is offering you. Beth Moore describes it this way, "Self-made fortresses not only keep love from going out; they keep love from coming in. Only God can put the pieces of our hearts back together again, close up all the wounds, and bind them with a porous bandage that protects from infection … but keeps the heart free to inhale and exhale love."[15] The walls you may build to keep pain out will never be too high for God. He has come to rescue you! He will scale the fortress and find you, but like a true gentlemen, He will not force Himself upon you. He will offer you His hand—the scarred hand that promises healing.

Healing isn't for some; it is offered to all! This may seem elementary on the surface but at the root of this truth is hope for us all. The sad truth is that even though it is *for* everyone, not everyone will accept it; but without Him, you cannot be made whole. He is the

One doing the offering. Which leads me to the inevitable question: How do we heal?

By his wounds, you are healed.

1 Peter 2:24 (NLT)

Our wounds are healed through His wounds. How is this possible? He's speaking about the wounds He received on the cross. We've heard the story, and perhaps we've even pictured that day in our mind, the day Jesus accepted God's call to walk toward His death like a sheep to the slaughter. He allowed them to beat Him, to bruise Him, to strip Him naked as they proceeded in whipping Him and pressing a crown made of thorns into His head; but they didn't stop there. The people laid Him on a cross, took each of His hands, and drove a nail through His palm and into the cross. Then they did the same to His feet. And after He died, just to make sure that He was really dead, a spear was driven into His side, piercing His heart as His blood spilled out before them.

Wounds. Did Jesus know about wounds? *Intimately.* But what is their purpose? Each wound was taken with joy for a purpose. Jesus knew that His wounds would offer us healing—emotional, spiritual, and physical healing.

Was His heart broken that day? Did He understand pain? Did He have a moment when His heart was shattered? I think He did. He had the weight of our sin on His shoulders—a sinless and perfect man carried the offenses of the entire world. God turned away from His own Son to allow His punishment to be poured out upon Him, but this forsaking was not in vain. Jesus died so we might live—so we might dance. Rising from the dead to conquer death once and for all was God's plan. This was Jesus's dance over His own ashes. A beautiful, triumphant movement accompanied with heavenly songs from on high. Jesus spun around, twirling and leaping as He stomped out injustice, sin, and death. He laughed as He danced over the enemy's vain attempt to keep Him in the ground and silence the life He offers to a misguided and dying world. At the core of His dance, the very reason He stood upon His ashes, was worship of His Father. In this dance, Jesus proclaimed that even in pain, when it seemed too much to bear, and when the enemy had left Him for dead, God had to be worshiped. Christ danced before His Father because He knew that in His own death and resurrection, others could experience freedom to dance. Have you been resurrected to dance?

WOUNDS

There are a few things I've learned about being wounded. The first: Wounds cannot be avoided in this broken and dangerous world. We will be wounded, and our hearts will be broken. As simple and as basic as this sounds, sometimes I need to be reminded that this world is fallen and corrupt, and because I dwell in this broken world, I don't have to go looking for pain, for pain will find me. Escaping is not an option. Even

Christ did not escape this fate. His perfect perspective now directs us in dealing with this hard fact of life.

The beautiful response to life's promise of pain and our enemy's attempt to fatally wound us on this journey is this: You don't have to remain wounded. Do you need to read that sentence again? You may *be* wounded, but you don't have to *stay* wounded. Healing is offered to all. Many times I'll be in the middle of a conversation with someone who is sharing their story with me, and I hear it in their voice. Their wounds, even though they occurred years ago, are as fresh as if they happened yesterday. I don't want to sound uncompassionate or uncaring, but what usually comes out is, "I'm so sorry that this happened to you, but why are you staying wounded?" It is a tragedy to live wounded because that is not what God has in mind when He says He has come to bring life. We can accept His offer to receive healing, or we can live chained to our injuries, licking our wounds like animals.

We say, "So if He's God, why did He let this happen? If He loves me then why didn't He save me or rescue me or fight for me?" That's where I was after my dad died. But God pointed me to the truth, even if I didn't like it. Trusting God at His Word may not seem easy, but it will save your life.

> "But I will restore you to health and heal your wounds," declares the Lord, "because you are called an outcast, Zion for whom no one cares."
>
> *Jeremiah 30:17 (NIV)*

Come, let us return to the Lord. He has torn us to pieces but he will heal us; he has injured us but he will bind up our wounds.

Hosea 6:1 (NIV)

How do we heal? From the inside out. You know how it works with a physical wound. It's got to be cleaned out. If you have a wound, and you close it up before it's been cleaned out, it could become infected, making it worse and turning it into an abscessed wound. If your wound becomes abscessed, it could take twice as long to heal, but the big danger is that it can make you really sick, affecting the whole body. An abscessed wound sounds a lot like an obsessed wound, doesn't it? If we live obsessed with our wounds, it creates the same internal decay and infection of the heart.

The first step in healing a physical wound is washing it out; but how do you "wash out" a wound of the heart? By the Word! Ephesians 5:26 says that we are "cleansed" as He washes us with His Word. Friend, Scripture says His Word is alive and active and penetrates us down to our bones. This Word will heal you. Don't be fooled by the world's counterfeit offers: television, friendships, sex, relationships, solitude, shopping, eating, fill-in-the-blank here. None can cleanse you and begin your healing process like the Word. Doesn't it sound ridiculous to think a large pepperoni pizza, a good movie or two, a new outfit, or pulling the covers overhead can heal us? I promise, these things can't heal. I've tried them!

I was broken hearted when I lost my father. I didn't

let God care for my broken heart or my wound, I just wanted to close it up and act like it wasn't a problem. But it festered, and I grew bitter and angry. I had an obsessed wound. I didn't let God wash it out and bind up my broken heart.

> My wounds fester and are loathsome because of my sinful folly.
>
> *Psalm 38:5 (NIV)*

That was my problem. And it wasn't until I opened and devoured the Word like I would a meal—partaking, digesting, being nourished, using it as fuel—that my healing began. If you believe that what is written in the Bible is true, even if you don't like it, you can challenge your thoughts and your heart when you want to hold on to bitterness, anger, resentment, or pride. You say, "I want to be depressed and angry that I've been hurt or that I'm having to go through this, but, Lord, Your Word says that 'never will You leave me or forsake me,' so I have to believe what is in Your Word over my so-called rights or feelings."

If you are currently in a season of your life where you feel wounded, I don't want you to hear me say that being wounded is necessarily a bad thing. Unfortunately, wounds are a part of living on this earth. But continuing to live wounded when God offers healing is *not* healthy or good. From the minute you receive a wound, He offers you Himself. His desire is to bring you in, "gather you in" closer, closer still, until He can wrap you up in His arms and begin the healing process.

BACK TO JESUS . . .

I am fascinated that in God's plan, Jesus dies and rises from the dead and goes around surprising everyone that He, in fact, is not dead but alive. But this is what gets me: Jesus, in His new body, comes back carrying scars from His wounds. The wounds that He received when He was crucified, the places where they put the nails and the place where a spear was thrust into His side still remained! I know He had a new body, a body that could pass through locked doors and show up somewhere in a moment—I understand that—but I wondered why He would still carry around His scars. I guess if I were writing this part, I would have had Jesus show up unmarked, like new. But no, He showed up in the middle of the disciples and looked straight at doubting Thomas and said, "Reach here with your finger and see My hands; reach here your hand and put it into My side and believe."

When I was wounded, I thought I had to forget my wounds existed so I could heal. I waited to feel untouched, unhurt, undamaged, and unharmed in any way. My wounds started to heal, but they left these ugly scars in their place. I learned that proof of our healing is in our scars. Jesus carried around proof of His wounds in His nail-scarred hands and sword-pierced side, and because of His scars, I see the significance in my own. Our scars give us opportunity to remember. It's not about obsessing over our past, or the opposite, acting as if our wounds never existed; it is about remembering them. I'm not wounded anymore. Scarred? *Yes.* I have scars that will never go away. Places on my heart that will forever remind me of the painful blows, the horrible nights, and the desperation and anguish I felt for months after my world crumbled. But these scars represent the promise of healing.

I wasn't "healed" just because God gave me the opportunity to be Dallas's wife. I wasn't healed when I found out that God had a man to be my husband or when I held my son Noah for the first time. I was healed when the Healer came near, and I said, "Yes" to Him. Yes as He gathered me to Himself and placed His scarred hand upon my broken heart and began to mend it. Yes when He used His Words to wash over my brokenness. And Yes when I stood among my ashes and danced even with tear-streaked cheeks.

Now I'm reminded of my wounds by looking at my scars, my battle scsars, as I like to refer to them. Why would we want to remember? Why show others your scars? Look what Jesus said, "Hey, Thomas, look at My scars. See My hands and My feet so you will *believe!*" Why do *I* share my scars—so you will *believe!* Why does Holly share her scars—so you will *believe!* Why should you remember your scars? To remember what God has done and how He accomplished the miracle in your life so you and those around you will believe.

God wants me to remember. That's one reason He called me to write this. But there are times when I can almost forget where I've been. Does that sound crazy? He's given me such a heart transplant that I can sometimes forget about where I've been and how bad my heart was broken. That's a testimony to His true healing power. At times, He points to my scars to remind me when I'm needing to find my way and says, *Heather, look and remember. Now believe!* Beautiful remembrances of a God that took my wounds and covered them with His scarred hands and said, *By My wounds you are healed!*

OUR TURN

Here's our challenge: love Him with more than just words. The call to dance has been presented and referred to in a spiritual sense, but I feel the need to take it one step further. I want to encourage you to take it further. I want to ask you to do something that might actually stretch some of you or make you want to burn this book, depending on what you are about to hear me say. There is something about expressing our worship to the Lord that pleases the heart of God and in turn changes the worshipper from the inside out. I want to encourage you to get alone with Him, lock yourself in your bedroom, or grab your iPod and find a field, just find a place you won't be disturbed and shut yourself up in a room and turn on some music that speaks of Him and of His goodness and just worship Him. In that moment, bring a sacrifice of praise (Hebrews 13:15). If your sacrifice needs to be a display of surrender, and you need to lift your hands, raise them high; if your heart aches, and your dance looks more like kneeling and singing through your tears, bring it all before Him. If you don't feel like it, friend, there's your sacrifice!

Maybe your sacrifice will include twirling and spinning, in adoration pick up those feet!

One of my favorite things in our home is our wood floor. I love to put on my socks and scoot around the floor for my Jesus! (Plus, Noah gets a kick out of it too!) There is something about being undignified for our God (2 Samuel 6:22). I don't have great rhythm—I've never learned how to two-step—but when our house is filled with His praises I can't help but want to jump around. And since I'm such a visual person, I try to picture Him there watching me dance before His throne. I'm sure I make Him laugh sometimes with my unco-ordinated but honest declaration.

One day in my Bible study, I met with some ladies from my church, and we got on the subject of dancing. And we recalled how some of us grew up in homes where it was unthinkable to even go to a dance. You were of the devil if you were even caught talking about it. One of the ladies shared how much they have always loved to dance, and they were always told how wrong it was, yet on Sunday mornings they had "dancers" that would come and dance on the stage. But they didn't call it dancing it was "creative expression." That was so confusing to her. If you have a hang up on that word or not, just remember King David dancing about undig-nified before his God. His "undignified" was without clothing! So my challenge to you: Be free! Dance! Where the Spirit of the Lord is, there is freedom (2 Corinthians 3:17). Make your worship a verb. Whatever the offering, make it a sacrifice offered to God and God alone. Don't hesitate—don't let fear or your own religious piety reign. Getting a little uncomfortable is good for us. Remember, dancing is a choice!

(If you need some song recommendations, I personally love the David Crowder Band, Hillsong United, Charlie Hall, and Nicole Nordeman, but I challenge you to find your own style and worship the Lord.)

ONCE UPON A TIME— FINDING YOURSELF AMONG THE PAGES

And in your book were all written the days that were ordained for me,

　　When yet there was not one of them.

Psalm 139:16 (NASB)

Do not boast about tomorrow, for you do not know what a day may bring forth.

Proverbs 27:1 (NIV)

Though you have made me see troubles, many and bitter, you will restore my life again; from the

depths of the earth you will again bring me up. You
will increase my honor and comfort me once again.

Psalm 71:20–21 (NIV)

For some reason I can't get past this analogy that God
is story, even though I hesitate to use the word *story*
because it implies a fairytale or book you read right
before bed that has a happy-ever-after ending. Even
so, it has been and is being written, and somehow in
His great mysteries He has chosen to give us an opportunity to share in its pages. It is a story that all others
derive from—a story that does have a happy ending.

When God asked me to stand before others and
tell my story, I didn't witness my own story emerge
but instead watched His emerge. Testifying about His
nearness during my desperation and grief did not lead
me to my own story but again to His. I struggled to
fathom why anyone would really want to read about *my*
experiences, but God clearly said, "This is My story!"
And that is why I write, not because I have *my* story
to tell, but that I have His. His Word says that He
has ordained my days, written in a scroll. I can almost
picture my life unraveling only as fast as He writes this
masterpiece. I picture His hand taking hold of His
writing utensil and scripting and constructing each
line, delicately adding His perfect touches to this wild
adventure. He carries out His wishes and His agenda
as He moves us through the day, through the months,
through the years. His personal tears accompany His
paragraphs, but He knows what must happen for us to
follow His path to the cross.

IN THE BEGINNING ...

The story didn't begin with us. God began our story by writing us into *His*. His is a story that has no beginning and no end. It's a story of the supernatural and eternal orchestrating divine intervention to make it possible for the depraved to taste eternity. Our wicked state was what paved the way to the cross. Our Creator sent His one and only Son to walk the road that led to death, and this death brought redemption and life to all who would accept this most honorable gift. It was a covering of blood over our corrupt hearts, minds, and souls. As His story unfolds, we find ourselves among the pages.

As He has unraveled the chapters of my life, there have been times I have been wooed by His love, taken by His grace, and enraptured by His Spirit. There have been moments I've found myself sitting on the edge of my seat to see what might happen next, and in others I've thought He threw in a surprise ending, leaving me for dead; yet through His mercy, the writing has gone on. Again, this is, in a sense, His story displayed through an ordinary life, a mere child of faith. By no means can you read that I am the main character in this novel. John Eldridge has beautifully articulated this concept in *The Sacred Romance* as he illustrates God as story and invites us to see the real hero of the story. "It is only when we see God as the Hero of the larger story that we come to know his heart is good."[16] This Hero has allowed my name to be written into the pages of His story. Your name is in there as well.

Beth Moore once said, "Who wants to read a book that doesn't have suspense and drama? It would be boring!"[17] God adds adventure to our lives not simply for adventure's sake but to speak more about Himself to the world—and to us.

I sit here somewhere among the pages of this novel, wondering what lies ahead. There are days when I'd love to skip ahead, but I can't. I can't rush the ending; I must enjoy the process of God revealing Himself along the way. It's not all about the destination but the journey. If we miss the journey, we won't be able to taste how sweet the ending actually is.

I want to share with you something that illustrates my point. This is a journal entry I made as I processed one life altering twist and turn in my journey.

October 1, 2006

> *Four days ago I learned about a new twist that He's added to my pages. A new life is growing inside me. I'm pregnant! Okay, now I'm crying. I guess they say that your hormones are extremely out of control and emotions seem to run high when you're pregnant. And all the moms out there shout, "Amen!" Well, the tears are fine with me. They actually speak volumes about my humbled state of gratitude and pleasure in taking on the task ahead. Am I scared? Most definitely! Am I sure that He has purpose in providing a twist to this adventure? Undeniably! I think about Mary when she first found out she was pregnant with the Son of God. She responded so beautifully to this over-*

*whelming news. She had no concern for her own
self; all she could do was respond in worship. Lord,
may I too have a heart that worships in response to
this most humbling call.*

Many of us don't respond to the twists and turns as
quickly as Mary. We question His purpose; we wonder
if we've heard Him right, if there may be some way to
get back to how things were. I guess the more and more
I live out this wild adventure I come to recognize His
ways; although, most of the time they seem foreign and
untamed to me, He has never once been wrong or has
not come through in bringing about something amazing. Although, through my skewed vantage point, His
twists and turns seem to throw me off balance or cause
me to struggle to take complete joy in embracing the
change, yet the Writer knows best, and I can trust the
Creator, the Hero of this story.

I've thought a great deal about where He's taken
me. I remember the moment I viewed the pregnancy test there in a stall at T.J. Maxx, a whirlwind
of emotions sweeping through me. But in-between the
moment that I thought for sure that I wasn't pregnant
to the confirmation before my eyes that I was, I was
reminded of what God has been about doing in my
life for some time. (I was also feeling quite foolish for
taking on this dare to check if I was pregnant in the
middle of our shopping outing!) For so long the Lord
would lead me through the book of Job to remind me
why bad things happen, how we are to respond, who
we are dealing with, and His intent on bringing about
not only restoration but retribution. I felt unworthy to

put myself in Job's shadow, but the Lord called me to stand there to take a good look at pain and desperation. The book of Job has been a source of healing for me as I read through the pages, hearing his anguish, feeling his pain, helping me to continually remember that I am not the only one who has ever felt this anguish. Not only did the Lord call me to take in Job's part in God's story, but He also called me to examine Job's ashes.

I looked at Job's crisis and into my own. Through the pain, I heard God speak to me. Just as Job has been an icon to those who suffer, he has also been a witness on behalf of God's goodness. Job witnessed firsthand what God was capable of, yet he also gained God's attention, being close enough to hear Him speak through the storm. Job watched as God revealed Himself. A first-hand encounter that would change Job's perspective on life and real living forever. How could love allow so much pain? Who is responsible for what has been taken? And if God is kind, then how can we reconcile kindness with these untimely deaths and all these belongings, once recognized as gifts from God, now taken or burned up in a moment? Later, it is again God's "kindness" that was shone as Job sat among the ashes, picking at his sores that covered him head to foot as his friends sat around accusing him of having some secret sin that triggered this outrage from God. Even through it all, God doesn't want us to miss seeing His own story. All attention is brought to the real story when God speaks. He begins by filling Job in on how things really work. He explains His power, His design, and His sovereignty. He puts the focus where it belongs—on Himself. He helps us get our eyes off of "Why me?" and onto "Who is He?" He never denies that He has seen all that has gone on even to the point of saying that He was, in fact, perfectly fine with all of it. But it is something in God's story and in His character that speaks volumes about Job's ashes.

God is very frank about His power, His sovereignty, and His rule over everything that goes on in heaven and on earth. He chooses to raise Job up and use his life's story as a promise of retribution to us. A promise that God is who He says He is and that He is justified in doing what He pleases with us, through us, and among us. God didn't have to explain Himself, bless Job by returning all that he had lost in double portion, or thwart Satan's plans by raising him up once again, but God knew that as He was writing His own story, Job would be among the pages, proclaiming God's sovereignty and blessings when we worship Him in the summer and in the winter.

You made both summer and winter.

Psalm 74:17 (NLV)

I know my pain had to be small in comparison to Job's, but I think anyone who finds him or herself in the path of a destructive storm asks the question, "Who is this God I thought I served?" Even though God showed Job who was boss, so to speak, God was pleased with how Job responded, which led the Lord to restore to Job what had been taken and also to remind Satan who's boss by blessing Job twofold.

Every time I read Job I had a hard time getting to

the ending. I got caught sitting among my ashes hearing God speak to me about His unexplainable otherness and my need to be okay with His character. I knew I needed to understand this before I begged God for His restoration and retribution. Was I at a crossroad, struggling for both control and a reconciliation of my false sense of reality? Yes. But here's where a new fear arose: I didn't want to get caught hoping that the end of Job's story would also be the end of mine and then be disappointed. Would God still be God if He didn't write my ending, in my opinion, as good and as beautiful as Job's? Would His love for me be any less if He didn't choose to show me the same grand finale? I knew the answer to that. Of course not. But you've heard that lie, haven't you? It has felt that way, hasn't it? If we don't have the earthly fairytale ending, then life is not "good."

At this point in my journey with Him, I by no means wanted to tell the Lord what to do; I knew His love was not in question, and I didn't want mine to be either, so to show my unconditional love, I resigned to be content in my circumstances, in my desperation, among my ashes. The struggle raged. I wanted to let my human nature run free. I wanted a fair and just ending. At times I wanted to selfishly grab the pen and take a stab at what I thought might be fair and just, but I didn't realize that if God gave me what I deserved, I would inadvertently earn hell. What I really sought was mercy—mercy to receive an "earthly" good ending.

Would God not bring about restoration in my life? Have you been there? The only thing that would bring us the most peace would be to hear that He will surely restore all that has been lost and that He'd never again pummel us with His wrath. I found myself needing a rainbow and longing to hear His promise to Noah, "Never again will I send my destruction down on the earth"; but those were not the words that spoke to my soul. He challenged my understanding of what "blessings" were and what the earthly standards were that my heart was so intent on receiving.

With our human eyes, we see our situation with a "worldly" vision, judging prosperity and blessings the same way those without Christ do, but His vision and His idea of blessings may look much different. Did He want to bless me? Yes, He told me so, but I found the real blessing early on, and it came in the form of a sweet relationship. He didn't want me to hold the "earthly" blessings higher than the journey—the one-on-one relationship with God Himself—that He was taking me on. During this journey, like I've said, I've been able to taste the sweetness of His blessings and recognize them to be God's handiwork. He made a promise to me that He was in the business of restoring and sending retribution on my land. I wanted that! But I knew that I couldn't miss out on the restoration He was doing in my heart moment by moment.

I missed precious moments. Many nights I sat among the ashes, wondering where my God was. When I lived alone, He promised me that I would again see restoration. But far more than He wanted to give me certain relationships to fill the void, He wanted to restore from the inside out. By His grace, I didn't miss the moment God gave me Hosea 6 to cling to in May of 2002. When I found myself in the dark, those verses were a light guiding me onward, promises I held fast to. While I was praying one night, He said, "Heather, I will bring about great and mighty things in your family, because of your love for me."

> Come, let us return to the Lord.
> For He has torn us, but He will heal us;
> He has wounded us, but He will bandage us...
> So let us know, let us press on to know the Lord.
> His going forth is as certain as the dawn;
> And He will come to us like the rain,
> Like the spring rain watering the earth.
>
> *Hosea 6:1–3 (NAS)*

He was writing my story, and this promise stemmed out of my love for Him. I was humbled and ecstatic that He knew of my love and that He wanted to respond in such a way. I knew that no matter what happened from then on, whether I was to ever be married again, have children of my own, or have a home with my name on the mailbox, He and I were lovers and in a relationship that meant more to me than any list could ever fulfill. The old way of thinking was disappearing, and I knew that what He wanted for my family and me was the absolute best. Why should I try to put a "worldly" spin on it and mess up His plan? There was nothing I could add to or take away to make His plan any greater, so I submitted my heart to "watch and see" what He was going to do!

And even as I have sat and tried to articulate this part of my journey, I see His face among the pages. For so long I would catch glimpses of God doing something amazing among my family but another attack would follow—another call with devastating news that Satan was still winning. I clung to this verse and held God to His promises. I have said many times, "God, You promised me that You were about doing great and mighty things in our family because of my love for You! When? Can it be now? Jesus, the painful reports are many surrounding my younger siblings. They are struggling and hurting; write the good into Your story now! Please!" More often than not, I found myself in the middle of silence; but I knew that the promise remained. I would open my Bible and there again, staring me in the face, was Hosea 6. His promise to heal, to bandage, to revive—and a promise to *know* Him.

But I have to say, I am glad that I am not the one writing this story because today, as I drink in the last few pages, I am amazed at the sweetness of our God. Along with most of my family, I desire for our family to be known as one that loves the Lord, and I am confident that others will see our family once again as a beacon and carrier of the Light. I don't want others to see destruction and pain; I want them face-to-face with a miracle.

A NEW CHAPTER

I grew up knowing I was a Wall. With that name came responsibility and recognition because of my father's role and reputation in the church but the enemy struck us down one by one. We were bruised and scarred. We wondered if we'd ever stand again, but today I see that God has rebuilt our home. Our "walls" now stand higher and stronger with a foundation laid by none other than the Ultimate Builder.

Today, Holly and Aaron live in Colorado where they are worship pastors of a rapidly growing church in the Denver area. They have witnessed God's story as they've stepped into His pages and worked hard for the glory of God's name. They lead hundreds in worship every week as a team. Everything they touch seems to succeed, and they have the blessing of favor with God and man. Their ministries have exploded as they write songs that their congregation uses to lift up God's name. They minister to various groups of people and give of all their energy and time to building up the church and their home. Their children: Emma, Malachi, and Ava are growing up in a home that honors the Lord and lives by the Spirit. God has placed them together to serve one another and those they come in contact with. I have witnessed few married couples that are making such an impact, and I sense that they've only just begun.

Heidi and her husband, Jacob, still live in Jefferson City, Missouri, where they are also living and giving of their lives to inspire hearts to follow Christ. Heidi is the worship leader at the very church we were raised in! This is the same church where our father served on staff for many years, and the same church that witnessed a divine miracle in his recovery. Some of the same people who prayed for our father's healing are there even today.

Heidi has walked through these years with such grace, holding our hands every step of the way, and God has molded her into a woman after His heart. Everyone who meets Heidi falls in love with her smile and passion for others. As a hair stylist, she has more than great hair. She uses her chair to share God's love with strangers and friends. Jacob, her high school sweetheart, is a manager with a cellular company where he is known for his genuine kindness and contagious personality. God's hand was in Jacob's life from the beginning, and God has brought beauty from ashes in his life by breaking unhealthy generational cycles that could have kept him from experiencing full life. They have two children, Avery and Sebastian, with one on the way.

In 2006 our mom married Bill, and it was so much fun to watch our mother fall in love again. Although we weren't ready to sit around hearing about their first kiss, God's timing and His part in orchestrating their meeting in Walmart on a Friday night, to the planning of their wedding four months later, mesmerized us. The family fell in love with Bill right away, and amazingly enough, we all knew him growing up because he and his family attended the same church in Jefferson City.

Bill and his first wife also experienced the same devastation as my parents due to unfaithfulness—under the same influence of the same pastor! Although my parent's marriage survived, the pastor's multiple affairs had been a part of the end of Bill's marriage. Who could have fathomed that God's story included a new partner for each of them thirteen years later and a love that grasped the need for forgiveness and new beginnings? After losing my father, my mom admitted that she desired to fall in love again but feared the moment she would have to tell the man she was to marry that she had been unfaithful in her first marriage. She carried such shame over the situation even after my father's death, but God had healing in His plan for her. He knew the man He had for her, and this man not only knew the pain of adultery but already knew my mother's part in it. Bill was faced again with reliving that same pain, yet he didn't hesitate to choose forgiveness and healing over pain. Bill extended that unconditional love to my mother, and God has begun a healing in our mom that we have waited a long time to see.

Our brother, Heath, now in his twenties, has experienced great pain over the years. At the crucial age of thirteen, Heath lost his father, and eight months later lost two of the men who were standing in the gap for him when Dad was gone. In the midst of frequent funerals and his own broken heart, he found himself in a house with a bunch of grieving widows. Heath's wounds run deep, and this void has led him down some dark paths full of disappointments and addictions. We all turn to something; I know because I've been there. Even so, in his eyes I see glimpses of the man God wants him to be. His talents are extraordinary, and through his ability to turn strangers into friends, we get to see glimpses of our father among us. Heath has begun his trek out of the dark. I pray for him continuously. Our family has felt incomplete during times that he has chosen to go his own way, living in opposition to the very One that is *for* him; yet God has continued to pursue him, and as Heath has begun to say "Yes" to God, I have hope to see this captive free!

My sister Hannah's story began without a father to call her own. Even during the time our dad was alive, he was struggling physically and most days admitted that he just wasn't himself. He left her world when she was only nine years old, and her early teen years ended up taking its toll on her—she most often chose peer acceptance rather than absolute freedom. Can anyone relate? But a few years ago she had a life-altering summer where she saw God pursuing her relentlessly. He is desperate for her to learn what it means to live out of love, not chained to her past but a chance to move forward with God as her protector. These are lessons most of us learn over and over on this journey with Him, but it's beautiful to watch God's love chasing her and calling her to more.

Hunter is the youngest of the bunch. He doesn't remember his father but longs to. His personality is exploding as he entertains us by playing guitar or shooting baskets out in the driveway. Before Bill was in the picture, there were days we would long for that father figure for him. The memory is fresh of the day when he was playing outside with his friends and came in crying because one of them had gotten mad and decided to hit him where it hurt most by saying, "Well, at least my dad's not dead!" Arrows pierced his already wounded heart. I think we all cried that day. But God's story included writing in a father figure for our sweet Hunter. Their friendship is developing, and Hunter is enjoying having a man he can look up to. Recently,

Hunter asked Christ to be his Lord; he acknowledged that he had said a prayer when he was younger, asking Jesus to come into his heart, but he said, "I don't think I kept Him there." He is being pursued and is responding! We can't wait to see what God has in store for him!

As for Dallas and I, our heads are swimming at all the change that has occurred in a matter of a few years. We have a beautiful boy named Noah. He came into our lives and has brought such laughter into it. He's always on the move, exploring and engaging in his world. I spend most of my days trying to keep up with him, but there are moments when he's still and quiet, and it comes over me—God's story! He has a plan for me, and it included my sweet Noah. Even the day Noah came into this world, we were reminded of God's love. Dallas was on the way to church, and he called me to tell me about the most incredible rainbow that stretched across the sky. I didn't know it at the time, but it was the exact moment that I went into labor. Yes, we had already picked out his name, but it was as if the Lord wanted to remind us that He was aware, sovereign, and longing to shower us with His love.

There have been moments as I'm rocking Noah to sleep and praying for him when all of a sudden emotion comes all over me, and God reminds me of His love for me. A demonstrative love of fighting for me that takes my breath away. A love that sings of retribution and of a Father that is good. After Noah was born, we began this tradition on Sunday afternoons of taking a family nap. Sometimes I wonder why we do this because we find out quickly that there is little room for everyone in one bed, but I try to cherish these moments because not too long ago this same bed was empty. Now we are all snuggled together like sardines. He reminds me in these moments of when I was too scared to dream of a moment like this, holding my child in my arms, and all I can do is love Him back. I whisper, "God, You are good. You are perfect. There is none like You! You were; You are; You will always be everything I need."

Dallas works full-time as a physician assistant, but God has blessed us with an opportunity to serve Him at LifePoint Church, in Ozark, Missouri, where Dallas leads our young adult ministry, and I'm a part of the women's ministry. We are having a blast serving along-side a humble and passionate pastor and friend as he leads our community, teaching men and women how to continuously learn what it means to love Jesus and love people—together. Dallas and I also serve on the worship team for our church. Music and the use of it to worship the Lord is a key component that the Lord has used in each of our healings, and we can't help but want to lead others in this way, pointing hearts toward Him.

I share all these things for one reason: to boast about Jesus. Yes, He was in the midst of my destruc-tion, and He is in the midst of this resurrection and transformation. He made a promise to me regarding my family; He didn't have to, but He did. I don't know all the reasons why He did, but I can surmise that the primary purpose was for His glory. Would I have loved Him and worshipped Him regardless? I pray so. Yet in His plan, resurrecting this family and receiving glory among our ashes was among His pages. He has and is in the middle of doing all that He wants to do in, through, and to us, so I continue to hold to that hope and promise.

YOUR PART IN HIS STORY

I don't know what your ashes consist of, what painful road you've walked, or the dark and lonely nights you've lived through, but I do know that God's story remains, and His story includes you.

> Being confident of this, that he who began a good work in you will carry it on to completion until the day of Christ Jesus.
>
> *Philippians 1:6 (NIV)*

This verse may be familiar to you, but don't read it lightly. Let it soak in and run through your veins; let His promise take root into your heart. To the naked eye, it may not seem like what you are going through would be considered a "good" work, but deep inside, you feel it, don't you? This unexpected nightmare may be the very thing that has opened your eyes to who it is you say you are living for. Like me, when everything was in flames and the dust cleared, I saw Him! Have you seen Him? Maybe your eyes met for the first time or maybe it was simply a more accurate encounter. Know that it is a *great* work that He is doing in you. The biggest shame is for us to go through our entire lives without catching a glimpse of God or experiencing what it means to have a real-life relationship with Him. That would be true devastation! And it would be to our demise!

> What has happened to me has really served to advance the gospel.
>
> *Philippians 1:12 (NIV)*

Whatever has happened to you has been done to advance the gospel. Paul wrote this after he had been shipwrecked, imprisoned, stoned twice, beaten up, left for dead, bitten by a snake, blinded, and the list goes on, and still he says that what has happened to him has been done to advance the gospel or move His story on. Paul found satisfaction in his sufferings because he saw the bigger picture—something worth suffering for, the most precious story that must be told of Jesus the Christ.

Oh, He has great plans for you! Plans to pull you into His chest and comfort your wounded heart, wiping your tears away and covering you with His love. You wonder if this love is just for someone else, if He could love you like that. You've said things, done things that have been adamantly against God or maybe you don't think He could accept you after all that. He wants you to hear this: "Neither death, nor life, nor angels, nor principalities, nor things present, nor things to come, nor powers, nor height, nor depth, nor any other created thing, will be able to separate us from the love of God, which is in Christ Jesus our Lord." (Romans 8:38–39 NIV)

Stop listening to the enemy and listen to the Way, the Truth, and the Life. The love is found *in* Him. Go to

Him; He will not reject you, for He is desperately seeking to bind up your broken heart, to comfort your grieving heart, and to move you from your ashes into a dance that will lead you into the rest of your beautiful story.

A DAY IS COMING

The day I was rescued from eternal separation between the Creator and His created was my day of salvation. "Now is the day of salvation" (2 Corinthians 6:2). You can be saved and rescued from living your life dead. Living dead looks like constant consumption without satisfaction. He can save us from our own agenda that leads us to a "chasing of the wind" (Ecclesiastes 1:4). King Solomon wrote the book of Ecclesiastes as a wake-up call to the rest of us. It is a cry to get out of the matrix and start living and loving life. In Solomon's reign as king, he ran headlong into addiction—not the addiction he was created for—but an addiction that fulfilled all worldly desire and any compulsive lust in his heart. This constant consuming resulted only in emptiness and a revelation that all was meaningless, a chasing after the wind.

For so long I must have looked so silly to God, running around in circles chasing the wind yet never getting anywhere. We are prisoners in need of someone to set us free. We are imprisoned to ourselves, evil desires, unmet wants, and you fill in the blank. And although we may be used to the way our cell feels and smells; we have something deep within us telling us there's more.

We desire freedom. We would all agree, but within our reality we may not understand what that looks like. We need someone that *is* Freedom and *is* Life to offer the key to our way out, One whose ultimate desire is for you and for me to really experience freedom and life. Salvation for so long has always meant to me salvation from hell. But what if it's about salvation here— for today? A plan to rescue us and give us eyes to see the world, not through the bars of our cells, but the beautiful opposite, a world without chains, bars, and unattainable rules. Will you let Him free you? I don't understand how we can choose our chains over His life, but it happens every day. The day of salvation is here! Will you cry out to be rescued?

A day is coming; it has been promised and told of in His story, and He will once and for all unite us with Himself. What will your story tell? Will it speak mostly of disappointment that has led to a life of resentment and anger? Have you confessed to know Him but remained comfortable in your cell, chained to a life full of pain and despair without healing? Maybe your shackles of choice have been unremitting grudges that control whom you are capable of loving. He has offered the prisoners, *all* prisoners, life eternal. An eternity that doesn't just start after you pass from this life to the next! Eternity now. Salvation now. An offer of eternal living today, stepping from old to new, having a new mindset, leaving the cell for good.

He reminds us that He plans to bestow upon us a crown of beauty instead of ashes, but so many of us choose to wear the ashes. We don't know how to move forward, so we throw ourselves a pity party and throw on more ashes to make sure everyone around us knows that we are in despair. God has come to set you free! This story that He writes offers a new beginning, which results in a different ending. What do you want your story to tell? If you've never asked Him to be your Rescuer, today is the day of your salvation! Call out to Him. Ask Him to be your Life. Leave your chains and follow Him.

He will come again, parting the sky and offering the one thing He is unable to offer at this time, His face. His hand and His heart, though, are offered now. Don't live among the ashes; draw near to Him, and He will draw near to you (James 4:8). Fear Him, love Him, and acknowledge that He alone is the healer of the brokenhearted. He may have torn you, but He will bind you up. You are living out chapters in a bigger story—a more important story. Find yourself among His pages, fill yourself with His joy, endure suffering, and express praise even through the dark valleys. Only by His mercy can we experience this life. My prayer is that you hear His voice speaking to you right now wherever you are. Don't miss what He is trying desperately to say to you! His love led Him to a cross to take on your chains, my chains, and the world's depravity, all to rest on His shoulders so you and I could experience the story we were created for.

Let Him write the pages that He desires; it will be beyond your wildest imagination: brilliant and perfect and accompanied by the Creator Himself. May we all take a deep look into who He is as He takes our hand in His and places it on His chest. Feel His heart beat for you. He is *for* you and desires to bring you through your ashes and into your dance. But He knows you can only experience pure joy when you've experienced pain. And we can only taste life when we've tasted death. He sees you. He is Love. He is an addiction. He is Light. He is Life. He is Dreamer. He is Redeemer. He is Story. He is Healer. He is...

May I have this dance?

Therefore we do not lose heart. Though outwardly we are wasting away, yet inwardly we are being renewed day by day. For our light and momentary troubles are achieving for us an eternal glory that far outweighs them all. So we fix our eyes on not what is seen, but on what is unseen. For what is seen is temporary, but what is unseen is eternal.

2 Corinthians 4:16–18 (NIV)

With our deepest
APPRECIATION ...

This book is written in deep respect and love for the ones that have finished the race before us.

Lord, we eagerly await the day we are reunited with our earthly Daddy, James, and Scott!

James

Used by permission: Fleming-Photo.

Scott

Heather

Dallas—You, my love, have stolen my heart. Thank you for your patient pursuit that continues even today. It is evident that you are a man that loves Jesus and that makes it easy to love and respect you. Wisdom and love flow from your lips, and they are the beautiful example of a life transformed by Christ. I am full of gratitude that He has asked us to walk together in this wild adventure, and I pray that our children follow your lead of loving God first and loving others as yourself.

Jim and Penny—I am so thankful for you both and have been so blessed by watching Him shine through your lives. You inspire me. Thank you for loving and embracing the new additions to our family.

Earnie and Loretta—God knew that I needed you! You have been such a sweet surprise as I not only married the most amazing man, but I married into a family that loves Jesus and loves me. You have been one of the sweetest surprises the Lord has given me.

Mom and Daddy Bill—Thank you for your support and encouragement as I share our story. Bill, you are truly a constant reminder of the perfection in God's timing and the fulfillment of His promises. Mom, I love you and am watching God do new things in you that inspire me to press in to Him more!

Holly

My "sweet" Aaron—You are the most wonderful and surprising gift in my life. The way you love our children, our great God, and me is a daily example and reminder of Christ's love for His bride. You are a man after God's heart whose drive to please your Creator calls me to higher levels of intimacy and understanding of Him. Thank you for your love and example in my life. I cherish you.

Mom Nesbitt—You are such a source of strength to so many. You love so passionately, and I consider it an honor to be a part of your family. Emma cherishes you and so do I.

Jim and Peggy—Where can I possibly begin with you two? I have never seen God so beautifully displayed in marriage and life like you portray. It's awesome to behold. Thank you for your constant love and encouragement and raising an incredible son.

Mom and "Papa" Bill—What a journey this has been for all of us. God has brought beauty from ashes for you too. God has done a wonderful thing by completing our family with a new earthly father. I love you both.

Heather & Holly

So many friends and family have prayed for us as we've embarked on this endeavor. Your prayers and encouragements have been invaluable! I want to especially thank my good friend Sarah Austin for using her gifts and skills in the preliminary editing of this work so others could make sense of our ramblings.

ENDNOTES

1   Rev. Lee Woofenden, "He is Risen," http://www.lee-woof.org/leewoof/2001/4-15-01.htm (accessed March 20, 2008).

2   Ibid.

3   "He's Been Faithful," Carol Cymbala, Word Entertainment.

4   "The Steadfast Love of the Lord," Robert Davidson

5   "Job," Cindy Morgan and Loran Balman, Word Records. All rights reserved. Used by Permission.

6   "This is How we Overcome," Rueben Morgan, Integrity/ Epic, 1999 Hillsong Music Australia. All rights reserved. Used by Permission.

7   Hannah Hurnard, *Hinds' Feet on High Places* (Wheaton, Ill.: Tyndale House Publishers, Inc. 1975), 26–27.

8   "You are the Sun," Sara Groves. Ino Records. INO Records, LLC. 2005. All rights reserved. Used by Permission.

9   Elisabeth Kubler-Ross, *On Death and Dying* (New York: Touchstone, 1997).

10   Oswald Chambers, *My Utmost for His Highest* (Grande Rapids, Mich.: Discovery House, 1992), 19.

11   *R.C. Sproul, The Character of God: Discovering the God who is* (Ventura, Cal.: Regal Books, 1995), 65.

12 Brent Curtis and John Eldridge, *The Sacred Romance: Drawing Closer to the Heart of God* (Nashville, Tenn.: Thomas Nelson Publishers, 1997), 158.

13 Max Lucado, Cure for the Common Life: Living in Your Sweet Spot (Nashville: W Publishing Group, 2005), 59.

14 Brent Curtis and John Eldridge, *The Sacred Romance: Drawing Closer to the Heart of God* (Nashville: Thomas Nelson Publishers, 1997), 156.

15 Beth Moore, "Straight to the Heart," Adapted from *Breaking Free.* (Nashville: Broadman & Holman, 2000). 110–114. https://www.lproof.org/StraightToTheHeart.htm. Used by permission.

16 Brent Curtis and John Eldridge, *The Sacred Romance: Drawing Closer to the Heart of God* (Nashville, Tenn.: Thomas Nelson Publishers, 1997), 82.

17 Quote from Beth Moore during Living Proof Live– Kansas City, Mo., September 9–10, 2005.